Sense and S

Deborah Ward is a writer whose passion for personal growth and psychology has led to the publication of numerous feature articles for a variety of print and online magazines, including *Psychologies*, *Natural Health* and *PositiveHealthOnline*. She is the author of *Overcoming Fear with Mindfulness* and *Overcoming Low Self-Esteem with Mindfulness*. She also writes a blog called 'Sense and Sensitivity' about high sensitivity for *Psychology Today* and writes blog posts about personality psychology for *Truity*. Deborah was born in England, grew up in Canada and now lives in Hampshire.

Photo © Kate Jackson

Contents

Foreword

It is a pleasure to recommend this beautifully written book to highly sensitive readers.

Having read so many books and much research on this topic in my 25-year career, I was delighted to find that the author has managed to truly capture the heart of what it is to be a sensitive person. By using touching, well-written stories from her own life to illustrate the real impact of living with this trait on her everyday experience, Deborah Ward describes both the struggles and the profound joys.

Along with engaging anecdotes, we learn factual information underpinned by reference to research, discover what it is to live a healthy, fulfilling, sensitive life, and reframe and uplift our view of sensitivity from something to be 'coped with' to something to celebrate and cherish. This book makes one want to hug the word 'sensitive' to one's breast and never let it go.

The world needs HSPs, just as they are, in all their wonder. Enjoy this book – I know I did.

Barbara Allen, founding director
National Centre for High Sensitivity CIC

Introduction

I'm eight years old and it's six o'clock in the morning on a bright, summer's day in small-town Ontario, Canada. We all pile into my parents' old green Chevy for the long drive to a friend's summer cottage for a barbecue.

I was born in England, but we emigrated to Canada when I was four and settled in London, Ontario, a small, leafy city with its own river Thames. We soon discovered that living in Ontario means going 'up north' in the summer, to cottage country, as often as possible, to escape the heat of the city and enjoy the great outdoors. Cottage country also means black flies that bite, mosquitoes and lakes full of speedboats and jet-skis roaring to the seventies rock melodies of Trooper and Rush.

It's a hot July day and I hear the gravel crunching under the tyres of our car as we pull into the driveway. As I peel my bare legs off the sticky, black vinyl seats, I notice at least a dozen other cars parked in front of the house. Several more line the roadside along the grassy edge of the woods. I can hear the throbbing music before I even open the door. I don't know why, but I suddenly feel nervous and my heart starts pounding. I jump out of the car and reach for my mother's hand. I quickly look behind me and catch a glimpse of sunlit triangles of surf on the lake, creating sharp points of light through the trees.

I can smell hamburgers cooking on the grill as we walk into the backyard. There are dozens of people there, all of them talking, laughing and shouting at the kids who run around the yard like squirrels. I cringe at their squeals and try to stand closer to my mother, pressing my face into her leg.

Suddenly I hear a shout and look up. A kid runs between two people and bumps a man's arm. He's holding a glass of water and he stumbles, takes a step forward and throws it all over me. I stand there for a second, trying to catch my breath, shocked by the cold and wet. I run out of the yard and back to our car in the driveway, shaking the door handle as I try to get in. But I can't open it.

I jump as I feel someone's hand on my shoulder and when I turn around, the man is standing there. He tells me not to worry.

'It's only water,' he says. 'There's no need to run off.'

He takes my hand and brings me back to the barbecue, where I dutifully try to smile and not spoil everyone's fun, and secretly feel that it's me who has done something wrong.

* * *

It wasn't fear or shyness or embarrassment that upset me about the water at the barbecue. It was overstimulation. I didn't realize it at the time, but I was feeling stressed by the noise, the crowds, the smells, the brightness, the heat and the enormous amounts of energy throbbing inside that backyard. It was overwhelming to me. When I was suddenly splashed with cold water, it wasn't just a funny surprise to be laughed about. It was a sensory overload, the last straw on my already heaving cart.

My overwhelmed response to this event arose because I'm a highly sensitive person (HSP) and I've struggled with this all my life. Sometimes, when I'm listening to music, walking in the countryside, or enjoying a deep conversation, it's bliss. I feel lucky that I can experience the kind of intense joy and passion that people sing about. But sometimes, it's tough.

What confused me as a child was that no one else seemed to be able to see or hear or feel things like I did. I never felt that I was overly sensitive. I felt normal. To me, it seemed like everyone else was strangely insensitive. How could they not notice the scent of the lilacs and not be bothered by the scream of a fire engine? No one else thought the music was too loud or the lights too bright. When someone felt upset, no one else seemed to notice, although I could see it and feel it as clearly as if they were shouting. I could see it in their body language, the slight downturn of their eyebrows or the way they rubbed their forehead, the tone of their voice, the way they put a cup down on a table, and the emotions that I could feel as easily as if they were my own.

Highly sensitive people have a sensitive nervous system, so we absorb and process more information than average and reflect on it more deeply. 'Information' refers to any kind of stimulus that the brain picks up through our five senses, such as sights, sounds, smells, light, colours, shapes, temperature, stress, energy and emotions. Most of the time, this is a subconscious process so we don't know it's happening until we feel saturated by too much input.

For example, HSPs can become overwhelmed when our environment is too noisy, too bright or too cold. We can also become stressed by large groups of people, chaos and clutter. We're often aware of other people's moods and feelings, to the extent that we notice them before they do and can feel those emotions ourselves.

Perhaps because we're so open to what's going on around us, we highly sensitive people experience the world the way a child does, as if everything is new and wondrous. Time moves slowly for children because they're constantly learning new things and they become absorbed in understanding them. Everything they see and do and hear is new and holds their attention. They are captured in the moment, as if time is standing still. This is why children are so often creative, and why artists have such a childlike sense of curiosity and openness about the world.

Being highly sensitive means you never lose that childlike ability to live in the moment. It allows you to maintain that sense of wonder and excitement about the smallest things.

High sensitivity makes you curious, playful, creative, open-minded and enthusiastic about the world, but it takes a toll. Noticing, absorbing and learning can be fun, but it's also exhausting and can be overwhelming. Just like children, highly sensitive people need a lot of rest and quiet time. And we need care.

But we can also care for others. Many sensitive people are insightful and have enormous emotional intelligence. We are highly attuned to other people, their feelings and their energy, and to our own emotions. Being sensitive and intuitive means we can understand and empathize with people deeply.

Still, it's not an easy trait to have in a society that values extraversion and sociability. Consequently, we can easily become convinced that we are 'wrong' in some way, and spend our lives trying to hide our true selves.

I started out trying to do what everyone told me to do. I tried to fit in. Life would be easier if I was like everyone else.

The trouble was that I couldn't do it. I often felt that there was something flawed in me or that I wasn't tough enough. I had heard people say to me things like, 'You're overreacting', 'Just relax!', 'Stop making a big deal out of nothing!', 'Don't be such a cry-baby!' and 'Stop being so sensitive!' so many times, I thought I must be doing something wrong. These negative beliefs become so ingrained that you're not even aware you're thinking them. But they affect everything you do, including the choices you make, the relationships you have, and your ability to pursue your goals and dreams. You don't even realize you're struggling until things go wrong. And then you blame yourself.

Many highly sensitive people struggle with low self-esteem, but that's not because insecurity is an inherent part of sensitivity. We learn to feel bad about ourselves when others don't accept us for who we are and as a result we don't accept ourselves.

It wasn't until I was 26 that I realized what was really going on. A friend gave me a book to read. Like me, she was a sensitive, creative person who noticed things. She didn't like crowds or noise. She was easily overwhelmed. The book was psychologist Dr Elaine Aron's *The Highly Sensitive Person*.

And that's when I saw myself for who I really am. I wasn't flawed or wrong. I wasn't weak or overreacting. I was just sensitive. I felt that I had been staggering around in the dark all my life and someone had finally opened the door. And I began to see that my sensitivity could be something positive. It could be something to cherish and to celebrate.

To find out if you are a highly sensitive person, you can take Elaine Aron's self-test in her book or on her website at <www.hsperson.com/test/highly-sensitive-test>.

I've spent years trying to understand who I am. It's an ongoing process. I can't say I've figured it all out or that I have all the answers, but I have learned a lot. My experiences have helped me to understand and accept myself, and I'm hoping they will inform, console, reassure and inspire other highly sensitive people to understand who they are, what they need and to feel good about themselves.

I'm also hoping that anyone who knows a highly sensitive person and has assumed they need to 'get over' whatever is ailing them will benefit from this book too. Wanting to do something to help the person you love is a natural instinct. But I believe the most loving thing you can do for someone is to try to understand them and accept them for who they are.

This book is a collection of stories from my life as a highly sensitive person, along with research and some suggestions based on things I have learned along the way. It's neither a biography nor my entire life history, but some anecdotes that illustrate significant moments and how I struggled, failed, adapted, learned, fell flat on my face, acted like a jerk, cried my eyes out, and ultimately found a way to live and thrive as a highly sensitive person.

This book isn't about how to overcome your sensitivity. It's about being true to your highly sensitive nature and the person you were meant to be – wired for wonder.

The science behind the sensitivity

Psychologist Elaine Aron coined the term 'highly sensitive person' in 1996. For many people, when you describe someone as 'sensitive,' it tends to have negative connotations, such as weakness, frailty or insecurity. They might think of a sweet, but vulnerable and fragile person who is prone to overreacting and fits of tearfulness – a cry-baby.

The scientific name for it is sensory processing sensitivity. It is an innate personality trait affecting approximately 20 per cent of the population. Researchers have found it in equal numbers in men and women. They have also detected it in over 100 animal species, suggesting that it may have evolved as a survival strategy, allowing certain individuals to be highly aware of their environment, and any possible dangers, and to reflect before acting.

Aron developed the acronym DOES to describe the major characteristics of high sensitivity:

- Depth of processing
- Overstimulation
- Emotional responsivity/empathy
- Sensitivity to subtleties.

Aron believes depth of processing, the tendency to process information more deeply, is the key trait of high sensitivity.

But the most noticeable behaviour is our tendency to become overstimulated and overwhelmed. This is because we're constantly absorbing sensory information. This may explain, in part, why HSPs are so often misunderstood. We can appear to be anxious, emotional and overwhelmed, but the causes of this behaviour remain invisible and unrecognized.

It is important to note that sensory processing sensitivity is not the same as sensory processing disorder (Aron 2016b). The former is not a condition or disorder but a trait that enables individuals to absorb more information from their environment and process information more deeply. Sensory processing disorder is a neurological disorder in which sensory information gets mixed up in the person's brain, resulting in inappropriate or abnormal responses. A groundbreaking study by Aron and her colleagues (Acevedo et al. 2014) proved that high sensitivity is not an imagined condition or a personality weakness. In her research, Aron found that people who score high on sensitivity have stronger activation of brain regions involved in awareness, empathy, attention, action planning, higher-order cognitive processing and responsiveness to others' needs. In other words, our brains work differently, more sensitively, than other people's.

Research by Bianca Acevedo and her colleagues (2014) also showed more brain activation in HSPs in the insula region of the brain. This area integrates understanding of emotions, body position and external events as they happen. Consequently, HSPs are more aware of what's going on, both inside ourselves and in the world around us.

Another study by Aron and her colleagues (2005) showed that feedback on a test affected the moods of sensitive students more than the non-sensitive ones, whether it was positive or negative, possibly because highly sensitive people care so much about the quality of our work, feel things deeply and reflect more on everything, including our own performance. We often try to prevent criticism by people-pleasing, putting others' needs before our own, or criticizing ourselves harshly.

Aron also suggests that high sensitivity is a genetic trait rather than learned behaviour and may be inherited. We are simply born this way. It's not a choice or a weakness or something to overcome. Sensitivity is often mistaken for introversion, but a study by Aron and Aron (1997) showed that it's unrelated. Similarly, it can be mistakenly confused with shyness, unsociability, insecurity, fearfulness, neuroticism, depression or anxiety.

In early studies, researchers saw high sensitivity as a vulnerability to mental health problems. But according to Aron, not everyone who is highly sensitive is depressed, so researchers began to look a little further, particularly because people who show signs of high sensitivity tend to do better than other people in positive environments and worse than others in bad ones. This is what's called 'vantage sensitivity'.

The term 'vantage' comes from having an advantage. Research by Pluess and Belsky (2012) found that when a highly sensitive person grows up in a positive, supportive environment, we perform better than non-HSPs in social competence, academic performance, health and other variables. But when we're raised in an unsupportive environment, highly sensitive people perform worse and can develop depression, anxiety, shyness and low self-esteem.

There's also a bias in Western culture against quiet, thoughtful and sensitive people. Our society values outward displays of strength and qualities like extraversion, gregariousness, decisiveness and low emotionality, so sensitive people are often misunderstood, bullied, rejected and told they are 'too sensitive'.

But other cultures greatly value sensitivity. A study by Chen, Rubin and Sun (1992), for example, found that highly sensitive schoolchildren were the most popular students in China, but the least popular in Canada.

Consequently, highly sensitive people can feel that there is something wrong with them and develop negative feelings about themselves. But it's not our destiny to live quietly hiding in fear. Nor is it our duty to try to act like everyone else. None of us is meant to try to suppress our true nature. Being highly sensitive can be challenging, but it can also be a gift. We need to use our talents and live the life that suits us, however unsocial or unusual it may appear to others. It's only when we embrace our natural abilities that we reach our potential, find peace and live the kind of life we deserve.

1

Overstimulation

'The individual has always had to struggle to keep from being overwhelmed by the tribe. If you try it, you will be lonely often, and sometimes frightened. But no price is too high to pay for the privilege of owning yourself.'

Rudyard Kipling

Christmas, 2009. I have just moved from Vancouver Island, Canada, to Leicester, England, which for most people in the UK sounds something like moving from Key West to Hackney. But Vancouver is a grey, stormy, soggy place in winter so I feel comfortable with the English weather. I was also unable to find a job on the island and found myself with the opportunity to fulfil my dream of living in England.

After landing a job and settling into my new home, I decide to drive to the shopping centre in Peterborough to do some Christmas shopping. I have never been there before, but I manage to find it with the help of my satnav. The shopping mall is big, with an enormous parking arcade and a multi-level, football-stadium-type building full of shops. I don't know why I thought this was a good idea, and I begin to regret it as soon as I walk inside.

The shopping centre in Peterborough isn't any different from a shopping centre anywhere else. It's a big, bright, place full of people and lots of things. In my experience, these places all tend to be pretty overstimulating.

As I walk around in a daze, dodging people with shopping bags, cringing at the sound of screaming babies and piped pop music, overwhelmed by the amount of stuff everywhere, I begin to feel like a rabbit on a highway. As I walk down the aisles, it feels as though the hordes of people walking around me are like speeding cars and I am a small animal, trying to navigate my way through this fast and furious concrete environment and somehow survive.

I forget all about the shopping and find myself simply trying to get through this experience. Everywhere I turn, there are bright lights, loud music, noisy voices, and the overwhelming avalanche of human energy coming at me from every direction.

I make it back to the parking garage, get into my car, shut the door and take a deep breath as the sudden silence envelops me like a blanket, and I burst into tears. It doesn't make any sense to me. I don't feel sad or angry or hurt. What does make sense is the feeling that for the last 45 minutes I've been trying to dodge endless oncoming threats to my safety and wellbeing. What makes sense is the same feeling I have every day – that I'm like a rabbit on a highway, a sensitive creature in an insensitive environment, trying to survive.

Oh, the noise, noise, noise, noise!

I'm sitting in the living room at home as a kid, watching television. My mum likes to read magazines and she's sitting next to me on the sofa. As she picks up her magazine, her fingernails scratch across the sofa fabric. It's the kind of thing that most people don't even notice. She doesn't do it on purpose. And she doesn't have extraordinarily long fingernails. She's just picking something up off the couch. But to me, the sound is excruciating, like nails on a blackboard. I cringe and tense every muscle in my body, raising my shoulders up to my ears.

My mum doesn't know that I'm a highly sensitive person or even that there is such a thing. Neither do I. I only know that I seem like someone who is overly picky and rather demanding. Someone who wants things a certain way. Neither of us knows that I just have a highly sensitive nervous system that makes certain sounds unbearable.

Machines do the same thing. Lawnmowers, hedge trimmers, leaf blowers, cars, trucks, motorcycles, jackhammers, vacuum cleaners, police sirens, fire alarms – they're all instruments of torture in my book. I'm like a horse that startles when you step on a twig. Most higher animals, including dogs, cats, horses, mice and monkeys, also have a wide range of nervous system arousal within their species. Around 20% of them are highly sensitive.

They're very aware of their surroundings. I'm the same way. It doesn't take much to make me jump.

It doesn't even have to be a loud noise. The sound of people whistling, humming, sniffing, coughing, snoring, throat clearing, gum cracking, pen clicking, foot tapping, chewing, slurping, whispering: all of it irritates me to the point that I'm often close to tears.

Cold comfort

At age 25, I'm dating a guy who loves baseball. He coaches a girls' baseball team and plays on his own team as well. He loves it so much, in fact, that he even plays in the winter. At this point, I'm living in a small town in Ontario, Canada, where winter is the real thing. We're talking snow, ice, below freezing temperatures and long underwear.

One weekend, Tom is participating in a baseball tournament, which means he'll be playing games all weekend. It is assumed by everyone that I will go and watch him play. I don't know whether I agreed to this, but somehow I find myself sitting in the stands on a bright, cold January day, wrapped in a fleece and a homemade hat, cheering him on.

Winter can be beautiful in Canada. When it's really cold, the sky is bright blue and the freshly fallen snow sparkles in the sunshine. Bare tree branches glimmer with ice, their long black limbs a skeleton frame beneath the frost. I love the sound of the snow crunching under my boots. Sometimes, when I walk in the woods, I find animal footprints that circle around and lead back into the trees, and I stand still and hold my breath, trying to hear them, unable to see them, like a secret.

At the baseball field, there is a concession stand where we can get coffee and hot chocolate, but it isn't enough. After one game, I'm sitting in the backseat of Tom's car, where I've come to change out of my wet socks, although I think I'm also hiding out here, finding some refuge in the silence of the frozen glass, away from the cheer of the crowds and the endless, heartless thwack of the ball. I am still shivering so much, I can't get my dry socks on. I hear a tap on the window. It's Tom, waving at me. I look away. He opens the car door and gets into the back seat beside me.

'Whatcha doin'?' he says.

'My feet got wet. I think my boots leak. I need new socks.'

'Okay. Well, the next game's starting in five minutes.'

My hands are shaking as I try to lace up my boots. It feels like the cold has seeped past my jacket, through all my layers of clothes, and into my skin, slipping deeper down into me until it's rushing through my bloodstream and grabbing hold of my bones, like tight fists.

'What's wrong?' he says.

'I'm... cold.'

'I know. It's freezing out there! But at least it's sunny. Do you want to borrow my gloves?'

'I've... got... gloves.'

'So why are you so cold? Come on, let's go back to the game. Everybody's waiting for us.'

'I'm not sure I can do this anymore. It's too cold for me.'

'I thought we were having fun.'

'We were. Well, sort of.'

'The other girls don't seem to mind.'

I take a deep breath.

'Come on,' he says, taking my hand. 'I'll get you a hot chocolate and we'll enjoy the game.'

We get out of the car and I zip up my coat, pull my hat down over my ears, and follow him to the concession stand, criticizing myself for not having fun.

The olfactory fix

One day when I'm about six, I'm enjoying a spring day out with my family. We've taken a walk along the river in Springbank Park in London, Ontario, where we live, and now we're having a picnic. I tell my mother I have to go to the bathroom, but when she takes me to the public washrooms, I refuse to go. I don't like the smell. And I don't think they're clean enough. I stand there holding my mum's hand. I'm not sure what kind of expression she has on her face at this point because my eyes are level with her waist. She explains to me that we don't have a choice, there's nowhere else to go. I decide to hold it until we get home.

About a week later, we're at our favourite local Italian restaurant, but before we order, I tell my parents I have to check out the facilities. This will become a kind of ritual as my younger sister follows me to the washroom for an inspection. But it's not always unpleasant. One of the benefits of high sensitivity is a deep appreciation for beauty and positive sensory experiences.

In this case, I find myself in a sanctuary of low lighting, soothing music, beautiful flowers, marble counters, lovely artwork, scented hand lotion and warm towels. I feel incredibly grateful and instantly relaxed. I can actually feel my heart rate slow down, my lungs fill with oxygen, my mind stop swirling. In this kind of environment, I am awash with a dreamy sensory bliss. I don't know how long we're in there, but I don't want to leave. Eventually, the door opens and my mother comes in, tells us we've been in here for ages and orders us back to the table.

Armed and dangerous

When I'm about 12, I go to a friend's house for a birthday slumber party. Fortunately, we are a bookish, soft-spoken bunch, so there is a minimal amount of squealing or gossip, and no eye-watering stench of nail polish. It is more like a tea party, which suits me. What I'm not expecting, however, is the filmfest of horror movies.

So we're all huddled together in our pajamas, eight young girls hugging pillows and giggling. Except I'm sitting with my face buried in my pillow most of the time, and the other girls are laughing at how frightened I am. I try to plug my ears during the movie so I can't hear the scary music or the screaming victims. I know it's just a movie, but my brain believes it's real. My sensitivity is absorbing every sound, every gory moment of the film as if I were experiencing it myself. I don't want to cry in front of everyone, so I hide my face in my pillow and try to shut it out, but I feel traumatized.

After lots of chatter after the film, everyone falls asleep on the floor, but I lie there all night, too terrified to sleep. When I go home the next day, I have nightmares for weeks.

Several years later, when I'm in my twenties, I go to the movie theatre with a friend to see *L.A. Confidential*. I don't know what the film is about, but I know that watching films at the cinema is even more intense because it's a big screen with surround-sound. It's meant to make you feel that you're experiencing it firsthand, of course, and it does. But there are some things I don't want to experience in person – like violence.

When we come out of the theatre, we bump into another friend of mine and they suggest we go for a bite to eat. But I can't move. I just stand there with my mouth hanging open, unable to speak. I feel as if I'm in shock. I'm numb, I can't say anything, I can't think straight. I look around at the people on the street and hear the noise of the cars whizzing past as if I'm still in the movie. At the same time, I feel as if I'm watching another world that I'm no longer part of. I can hear my friends talking, and see their lips moving, but I can't say anything. It's as though I have post-traumatic stress disorder but no one can understand why.

My friends keep talking and throw disapproving glances at me and then decide to call it a night. Someone puts me in a car and takes me home.

I still can't watch scary movies or anything violent or upsetting. I can't watch the news. If an advert for the Humane Society or the Donkey Sanctuary comes on television, I have to change the channel. If I watch, I will be in tears. I'll have nightmares. I don't avoid these things because I don't care. I avoid them because I care so much; I can't bear to watch. What other people consider normal, I find upsetting. What people call edgy, I call traumatic.

The hell that is shopping

Saturday, 10 a.m. Must get to grocery store early to avoid weekend crowds. This is England, so naturally it's raining. But I'm prepared. I'm wearing my waterproof jacket with the hood up. Find parking spot. Get reusable, environmentally friendly shopping bags from boot. Find shopping cart. So far so good. I enter the store and discover my cart has a squeaky wheel. And so it begins.

The supermarket is a big place with bright lights, and there are lots of people moving in different directions, talking and laughing. Babies are crying, children are whining. Tinny Top 40 music is playing overhead, interspersed with nerve-rattling employee announcements. I fear this will only get worse as Christmas draws closer. When they start playing 'I Wish It Could Be Christmas Every Day', I plan to wear earmuffs. Or a helmet. Possibly combat gear.

The shelves are filled with thousands and thousands of objects in all different shapes and sizes and colours. My brain is soaking it all in, every last detail.

I've got a list so I shouldn't be too long. That's the plan. But I can't find the dill. I ask a store assistant where it is and he tells me it's in the last aisle. I wheel myself around and down the previous aisle. Squeak, squeak, squeak. I can't find the dill. I ask another assistant. He says the dill is in the next aisle. I take a deep breath and push my cart back to where I'd just been. Oh, he says. Looks like we're all out of dill.

An elderly couple stand in the middle of the aisle discussing mayonnaise. I say 'Excuse me' and smile and wait. They haven't heard me. I say it again, slightly louder this time, but they don't budge. I try to manoeuver around them, and apologize for bumping their cart.

By the time I've made it out of the fruit and vegetable section, I'm feeling overwhelmed. I'm no longer walking but staggering, no longer pushing my cart but clinging to it. My mouth is hanging open and I haven't blinked in ten minutes.

I need to do things a bit more slowly than other people because I'm constantly absorbing and processing everything around me and it's overwhelming. Everything makes me think and form connections and triggers my curiosity into asking questions. Sometimes I'm aware that I'm thinking about other things, such as when the picture of the farm on a jam jar label reminds me of the apple orchard where I grew up. I wonder if it's still there? But I'm also soaking up the information around me unconsciously. Nobody likes to be rushed, but the sensory overload makes me feel rattled, like dice in a cup, shaken up and tossed out.

I finally make it to the check-out aisle, where I stand numbly waiting. In the next line, a child starts screaming. She's just a toddler and she's probably tired or hungry or, like me, has just had enough. Something inside me leaps up with empathy for her. But the sound of her crying is ear-piercing and my eyes fill with tears. It feels as if someone is screaming into my eardrums. I try not to cry, but I'm shaking.

I get out of the store and then out to the parking lot. I load everything into my car and then get in the driver's seat and shut the door. Suddenly the windows fog up and I can't see anything. And no one can see me. My hand is shaking as I put my key in the ignition and burst into tears. I decide that I will start shopping online and get my groceries delivered.

Making sense of sensitivity

While overstimulation is not the primary trait of high sensitivity, according to Elaine Aron, it is often what we notice most. Life as a highly sensitive person is a life with the volume turned up high. The daily onslaught of information from the world around us can be a constant source of stress. We feel overwhelmed by emotional, social and sensory stimulation because our brains absorb more information, process it more deeply, are more aware of subtleties and are more emotionally responsive. And, says Aron, we get more sensitive as we get older, both HSPs and non-HSPs alike.

I'm particularly sensitive to noise, temperature and people's emotions. Lights also seem to be turned up too high. I never use ceiling lights in a room. I always use lamps. I replaced all the lightbulbs in my house with environmentally friendly low-light lightbulbs. The whole place whispers in a soothing crepuscular glow. Many offices use those long, fluorescent light tubes in the ceiling, which have a tendency to flicker, buzz, and cause eye-strain. Unfortunately, there's not much I can do to change the lighting at work. I just try to get outside as much as I can, and at home I keep the light low and use candles.

Candles, fireplaces and campfires can all make us feel more relaxed. Research by an anthropologist from the University of Alabama (Lynn 2014) revealed that our blood pressure decreases and we become calmer when we look at flames. This may have originated from our cave-dweller days of gathering around a fire for warmth, safety, food and comfort.

Similarly, highly sensitive people can be sensitive to artificially scented products, perfume, cosmetics, cleaning agents, detergents, paint, chemicals and cigarette smoke. I enjoy pleasant aromas like flowers, the smell of cut grass and fresh peaches. They don't bother me. But some artificial scents like potpourri and scented candles give me headaches. Many HSPs suffer tremendously from environmental sensitivity to scents, resulting in headaches, coughing, muscle aches, breathing difficulties, confusion and fatigue.

Highly sensitive people vary in the degree and the types of things that we are sensitive to. Some highly sensitive people may be more affected by texture, so they're overwhelmed by annoying labels in clothing or scratchy fabrics. Some may be sensitive to different kinds of sounds or smells or stimulation. But the feelings we experience as a result are the same. And despite our attempts to fit in and to try to adapt and keep trying, eventually we reach a point where it all gets to be too much.

Despite this ongoing battle with sensory stimulation and feeling overwhelmed, most highly sensitive people are unrecognizable in public. You generally won't see us crying, melting down, having a temper tantrum, or behaving like a three-year-old. We've learned from an early age that life is about survival, so we keep our heads down and push through until we know we're on safe ground. It's usually not until we're in that safe place that the stress of the overstimulating environment reveals the toll it has taken. Sometimes I'm not even aware of how stressed out I am, or how overwhelmed I really feel, until I get somewhere quiet and it all comes tumbling out.

Some highly sensitive people have spent so much time in survival mode, just trying to cope with the endless harassment of everyday life and trying to bury their sensitivity, that they can never really let go. They're always on 'high alert', always watching for danger in the form of bright lights, loud noises and crowds, but never really taking the time they need to relax or just be themselves. There always seems to be another source of overstimulation.

I know I'm on high alert when I go to places like shops or airports. They are packed with sensory stimulation and I tend to rush through them in a 'fight-or-flight' state of mind. I feel so overwhelmed that it seems as if I'm struggling for my survival, usually with my mouth hanging inelegantly ajar and my eyes unblinking in some perpetual state of shock.

This sensory overload is why highly sensitive people tend to retreat to quiet places or stay at home. It's not that we don't like people or that we're shy necessarily. We just find them and the world they live in overwhelming sometimes. When I have absorbed too much, I feel saturated, like a soaking wet sponge, unable to absorb any more.

A study by Zabelina and colleagues (2015) found that highly sensitive people have what they call 'leaky sensory gating'. Sensory gating is the ability to filter out stimuli from the environment that the brain considers unnecessary. It helps us to focus on what we need in order to survive. For an HSP, that gate is 'leaky,' so a lot more information seeps through.

I personally think that 'leaky' isn't the best way to describe what's happening as it suggests that something is leaking out. In fact, we are absorbing information, so instead of leaky gating, I would say it's more like having gates with a lot of holes in them. Consequently, everything comes rushing through our gates and into our brains, and since there's no barrier to stop it, we feel overwhelmed. Our brains just don't have a filter as non-HSPs do. This is why too much noise, violence, smells, energy and emotion can be stressful to highly sensitive people.

But the researchers also found that one of the benefits of having such 'holey' gates is increased creativity. Since the brain tends to absorb only the information it needs, absorbing more can allow us to make connections between seemingly dissimilar elements and form new associations. In other words, absorbing more information lets us be more creative. And to be creative, highly sensitive people need a balance between stimulation and reflective solitude.

When we do get the downtime we need to recharge our batteries and avoid overstimulation, we recover, feel restored and can begin to use all that information in creative ways. Our experiences can also give us a chance to learn better ways to cope and a better understanding of who we are and what we need.

What I learned

Becoming overwhelmed by sensory, social and emotional stimulation is a common effect of being highly sensitive. Here are some of the things I have learned that can make it easier to cope.

1 **Look after yourself.** I've learned that as a highly sensitive person, I'm both the curious child and the parental control. I have to monitor what I allow myself to watch on TV. Consequently, I don't watch anything that would be unsuitable for a very young child. I also have to take care to avoid subjecting my sensitive self to overstimulating activities that most people find fun, like Formula One car racing, family-friendly community events, rock concerts and shooting parties. We HSPs need to protect our sensitivity and nurture it. It needs looking after and it needs cherishing. It can be demanding at times, but when we see our sensitivity as a child and ourselves as the parent, it's easier to say no to anything that might hurt our sensitive nature.

2 **It's okay to cry.** Highly sensitive people experience a lot of sensory and emotional stimulation and, consequently, we need to release all that energy. It's more culturally acceptable for women to cry, but HSP men and women alike need to give themselves permission to express their feelings. I don't like to cry in public, but when I get home and let it all out, I feel better. Don't hold it in and try to be tough. Feelings don't disappear just because you ignore them. In fact, they tend to build over time.

   I've found that the best way to get over any stressful event, whether it's a noisy shopping trip, a divorce, or a bad day at work, is to cry, talk, write, and cry some more until you can't cry anymore. It's the only way to let it go. Fortunately, I can't seem to hold my feelings in even if I try. I believe it's one of the benefits of being highly sensitive – being naturally emotionally responsive means I can deal openly and honestly with my feelings. While many people may believe that showing your feelings means you're weak and *controlled* by them, I find the opposite is true. Expressing your feelings *releases* you from the stress and pain of your experiences, enabling you to move on unencumbered.

3 **Take breaks.** If you work in a busy, noisy or stressful environment, your sensitive brain will quickly feel overwhelmed and you may become tearful, irritable, anxious or depressed. While we can't

always change jobs, we can try to take regular breaks during the day and go somewhere quiet for a moment of peace to soothe our rattled nerves, whether it's a quick walk outside or simply a trip to the office washroom.

4   **Get organized.** Just as children flourish with a regular routine, your sensitive side will cope better when you have a plan. If you have a big meeting at work, try to schedule some easy tasks you can do alone afterwards so you're not overwhelmed all day. Leave plenty of time to get to events so you're not stressed by rushing or searching for parking. Arrange your own transport so you can leave when you want to and avoid signing up for too many activities at once. If people criticize you for not participating, just tell them you need some downtime. People who really care about you will understand and respect that.

5   **Eat well, and regularly.** Busyness, being around people and absorbing information, takes a lot of energy and HSPs can quickly become exhausted. Keep your strength up by eating regular, healthy snacks and meals.

6   **Get plenty of rest.** While we cannot always take a nap during the day, we need to make downtime a priority. Looking after our sensitive self means ensuring that we get enough sleep at night. I try to get eight hours a night and take some regular quiet time just to reflect and recharge. Absorbing information all day is like learning. It's stimulating but it's tiring.

7   **Be aware of your feelings.** Knowing what you need means listening to your own mind, emotions and physical reactions. Notice when you're feeling anxious, depressed, cranky or emotional. Do you get any physical symptoms, like shaking hands, a racing heart or crying? If you've been busy or overstimulated, it usually means your sensitivity is overwhelmed and you need some quiet time. For me, spending time in nature or listening to relaxing music is one of the most soothing things to do to recover.

8   **Spend time alone.** HSPs need a lot of time to unwind, especially after a particularly noisy, busy or stimulating event, such as a meeting, a day out in a city centre, spending time at an airport or, of course, shopping. While spending time with others can be fun, people are also very stimulating. Research (Doherty-Sneddon and Phelps 2005) shows that just looking at someone's face is so

interesting to the brain that we often have to look away to reduce the cognitive demand so we can focus our thoughts.

Any place where there are more than three people will generally overwhelm me. It doesn't take much. Spending time alone recharges my batteries and soothes my nervous system. I like to read, write, listen to classical music, watch documentaries and take long, solitary walks in the countryside. When I spend time doing these things, I feel calmer and ready to face modern life again. People may think you're antisocial, shy, lonely, afraid or just plain weird, but you have to do what's right for you. It really doesn't matter what anyone else thinks. Spending time alone is not a luxury, but a necessity.

9 **Shop online.** Seriously, online shopping was designed for highly sensitive people. You can avoid the crowds, the noise, the lights and take your time. I don't need to squeeze the tomatoes or chat with the checkout lady. If I do go to a supermarket, I wear headphones and listen to music. It looks a bit strange and is perhaps fairly antisocial, but I'm not there to make friends. I'm there to do a job and I need to get in and get out as fast as I can before I get sensory overload. I've got a shopping list, and I'm not afraid to use it.

2
Awareness

'Let us not look back in anger, nor forward in fear, but around in awareness.'

James Thurber

I'm about ten years old when my mother takes my sister and me to visit a friend and her children. There are three of them and they're about our age, my mother assures me. I've never met them before so I'm apprehensive. We're all sitting around in her backyard when her kids suggest we walk down to the local baseball field and play catch. It's a dry, hot summer day and I can sense that the grown-ups are eager to get us out of their hair for a while. I am not, nor will I ever be, a sports enthusiast, however, so I am not thrilled with the idea. Plus, I don't know how to play baseball. But I dutifully tag along with the others, their bats and balls bouncing over their shoulders.

At the baseball diamond, the others talk about who will be the pitcher and who's first up to bat while I stride out to left field. Way, way out. We start playing although I have no idea what's going on or if my team is winning. I'm not even quite sure which team I'm on. I only know I have to duck when the ball comes towards me. I know that's not what I'm supposed to do, but it seems like my best chance of survival. Besides, standing out in the field gives me a chance to look at the trees and the wildflowers and the clouds drifting across the sky. I'm watching the way the breeze brushes the leaves of the trees that line the edge of the baseball field when another group of kids comes over. Shielding my eyes from the sun with my hand, I see someone wave me in. So I slowly walk back toward home plate.

The other kids are a group of three or four boys about our age. They ask if they can play ball with us. The others happily agree and they all spread out and find their positions on the field.

'I'm going home,' I say to no one in particular. 'I don't want to play anymore.'

No one is surprised, but they're all unimpressed. I'm acting like a spoilsport and ruining everyone's fun again. As usual. No one encourages me to stay, but I can feel their eyes rolling and their heads shaking as I walk away.

Back at the house, I sit down in the backyard with my mum and her friend.

'You're back early. Where are the others?'

'They're still playing. I didn't want to play anymore.'

'Why not?'

I look at my shoes. My long white socks have fallen down and pooled around my ankles. I shrug.

'Did something happen?' asks my mum's friend.

I shake my head. 'We were playing and then these other kids came over and wanted to play. I didn't want to play with them. I didn't think they were very nice.'

'Why? What did they do? Were they mean?'

'No.'

I don't know how to explain it. I don't say anything more. I know it doesn't make sense and I'm sure that my mum and her friend think I'm just overreacting or that I'm just too shy to play with boys. I hardly know why I don't want to play with them. I only know I don't. So I sit with my mum and her friend while they talk about boring grown-up things and I drink lemonade, feeling like an outcast and not knowing why.

About half an hour later, the rest of the kids come back.

'How was the baseball game?' my mom's friend asks.

'It was okay,' says her oldest girl, leaning on the back of her chair. 'Well, it was fun. But then these boys came over and wanted to play with us. It was okay at first, but then they started telling us what to do and wouldn't play by the rules and acting mean, so we left.'

I sit quietly clutching my glass, knowing that no one has made the connection between those boys and my leaving the game early. No one but me. And I have no idea how or why I knew something was wrong, but I knew it was.

Making sense of sensitivity

Highly sensitive people are very aware of subtleties. We're very perceptive and aware of details and changes in our environment. We notice things, both consciously and unconsciously. That includes everything from the way the light falls on a patch of grass to the way people are feeling, to what they're wearing and, sometimes, their motives and intentions. We're highly attuned to other people's likes and dislikes, to their needs and desires.

This awareness has allowed me to notice things that other people don't notice. For example, at one job, I noticed that my boss would rub his face whenever he felt stressed. It seemed so obvious to me, I couldn't understand why no one else recognized it.

I've noticed people singing when they are worried, clearing their throat when they're unsure, whistling when they're nervous and the ever-popular pen clicking – a sign of anxiety. Many people have these kinds of unconscious habits that tell me what they're feeling. They are behaviours that we unconsciously use to alleviate stress, giving people an outlet for their nervous energy and making them feel calmer. But let's face it, they drive highly sensitive people round the bend.

Highly sensitive people pick up on less obvious cues as well. For example, I was visiting my parents one day when they had some friends over. They had known this couple for quite a long time and they had always seemed happy to me. We were all sitting in the living room of my parents' house, drinking coffee and talking. They didn't say anything unusual and they didn't behave any differently from normal, but I felt that something was wrong. Jane was unhappy. I could feel it.

After they'd left, I asked my mum if she'd noticed there was something wrong. She said she hadn't. But later that week she got a phone call from Jane saying she'd been worried because her sister was ill. I'm not psychic. I was just aware of her feelings.

I think awareness of environmental stimuli also tends to make highly sensitive people more considerate of others. We hear those annoying pen clicks, we smell the person bathed in cologne, we back away from the loud talker. And in the face of all this noise and distraction, we think that other people must be bothered by it too, so we try to minimize those things for other people. Consequently, highly sensitive people are often very considerate and possess great emotional intelligence skills that serve us well in both personal and professional relationships.

Of course, we also tend to find a lack of politeness and courtesy in other people rather upsetting. My intense awareness of my surroundings can make it hard for me to understand why anyone else wouldn't show the same consideration. Running along the sea wall in Vancouver a few years ago, I saw a couple walking towards me with a little dog. They had one of those extension leashes that lets the dog run on a line while the owner doesn't have to move any faster than a snail. Unfortunately, they let her rip just as I was running towards them, the lead extended across the width of the sea wall and I was clotheslined.

In a study with her colleagues (Jagiellowicz 2011), Elaine Aron tested a group of highly sensitive people on a change detection task while undergoing functional magnetic resonance imaging (fMRI). Sensory processing sensitivity was associated with significantly greater activation in brain areas involved in visual processing, as well as in the right cerebellum, detecting minor changes in stimuli. These findings were true whether the subjects were introverts, shy, anxious or not, indicating that these characteristics are not an inherent part of being an HSP. What is inherent is the tendency for HSPs to notice, absorb and process information more deeply.

What I learned

Being highly aware of your environment and the people in it can be exhausting, but it can also be exhilarating and breathtakingly beautiful. Here are a few things I have learned about this balancing act.

1 **You're not crazy.** And don't let anyone try to convince you that you are. There's nothing wrong with you. You're simply born with a brain that absorbs details. For years people told me to stop being so sensitive, as if it were something I could control. I didn't know then that it was an innate trait. But I do now. And I know I'm not too sensitive. And neither are you.

2 **Put your needs first**. Most of us have a hard time with this idea because it feels selfish and we've all been told to think of others before we think of ourselves since we were children. And while you shouldn't ignore other people's needs, you need to look after your own as well. There needs to be a balance. It's okay to say no to something that others call 'fun' but you know will wear you out. And it's okay to avoid people who drag you down. You need to look after yourself.

As I've developed an increasing awareness of my sensitivity and what rattles me, I've tried to structure my life around it. I've been fortunate to find jobs that allow me to work at home part of the time. This allows me time and space to work quietly, on my own, and to have more control over my environment. I keep the lights low, play soft music and enjoy the quiet.

3 **Trust yourself**. Highly sensitive people are not psychic. We can't read people's minds or predict the future. But we are very intuitive and emotionally aware, so trust that. Just because no one else is aware of something doesn't mean it's not real. If something is too loud, too cold, too bright or too anything for you, that's reason enough to do something about it. You can't always change your environment or leave a situation, but you can often make things more comfortable for yourself. And if you get a sense that someone is untrustworthy or deceitful, trust that too.

4 **It never hurts to ask**. It can be easy to feel trapped in situations that frazzle you and to feel stressed, angry and resentful about the seeming lack of other people's awareness of sensory stimulation. But most people are not highly sensitive and so they are simply unaware of the stress they may be causing. If something in your environment is overwhelming you, it's up to you to try to fix it. Don't just sit there and feel sorry for yourself. You can't run around pulling down blinds and turning up thermostats, of course, but it never hurts to ask. Working at home, for example, is becoming more the norm these days, so just ask your employer if this might be an option for you. You will probably be much more relaxed and more productive.

I used to work in an open-plan office, which was like trying to concentrate in the middle of Disney World. One of my colleagues liked to scroll with her mouse, but it was very noisy and sounded like nails on a blackboard to me. So I sent her an email and explained that I was very sensitive to noise and asked her if she would mind using the up and down buttons on her keyboard instead. She was completely unaware of how loud her mouse was, and since I suggested it was my sensitivity and not her fault, she said yes, no problem. *Voilà!*

5 **Love yourself.** Many sensitive people become cautious, anxious, fearful and insecure because of their experiences of being criticized, rejected and overwhelmed. We can begin to hide ourselves away and lack the confidence and assertiveness to pursue our dreams or to stand up for what we believe in. But knowing what works for us and what doesn't, and sticking to those boundaries, can help us to feel good about who we are and to remember that our needs and opinions matter. Because highly sensitive people are more aware of our surroundings and our own feelings than other people, we tend to have a better understanding of when we are stressed, overwhelmed and what we need to feel calmer, allowing us to face difficult situations rather than pushing them away. The more we understand this trait and feel good about being a highly sensitive person, the more confident and happy we will be.

6 **Love your gift.** While being highly aware can be overwhelming, it can also be a treasure. I feel incredibly lucky to be so aware of the beauty all around me. I'm always aware of the way the clouds move across the sky, the sound of the wind sweeping across a field, the beauty of sunlight reaching its bright fingers through the trees. I often wish other people could see and experience things the way I do. It's almost as if I'm wearing special glasses that let me see things that others can't. Perhaps the best part of being highly aware is my ability to feel other people's positive feelings. I've been in a room where everyone is happy and I can feel absolutely punch-drunk with joy. When someone else is excited, relieved, happy, rewarded, victorious or successful, I can feel it. And I wouldn't change that for anything.

3

The sensitive body

'Our own physical body possesses a wisdom which we who inhabit the body lack.'

Henry Miller

I'm 24 and living in Toronto. One day at lunch, I bite into an apple and feel a strange sensation in my mouth. My tongue is itchy, my throat is sore and my lips and gums start to swell up as if I've been injected with Botox. Fortunately, the swelling and itching go down as soon as I swallow some liquid antihistamine.

When I was growing up in Canada, we lived not far from a farm with an apple orchard. Every autumn, we'd fill our baskets with Red Delicious and Pippins, so that we had an apple in every lunch box, apple pies for dessert and home-made apple sauce.

I don't eat apples anymore. I've also discovered that I can no longer eat raw pears, plums, peaches, nectarines, kiwi fruit, grapes, carrots, celery, almonds, peanuts or walnuts. I can't be in the same room as raw potatoes, as I discovered while making a shepherd's pie, when I developed an allergic reaction to them like I was standing in a hay field on a windy day. I was told that it was not an allergy to pesticides but a sensitivity to the pollen of a plant or tree. Fortunately, I can eat any of these things cooked. Nothing like a nice cooked plum on a summer's day.

I'm not sure if I'm getting more sensitive as I get older, or just becoming more aware of my sensitivities, but you can't deny the reality of swollen gums and a tongue rash. There's something about physical symptoms that really makes you wake up and take notice. It's as if my body had finally had enough of my wallowing self-pity, denial and self-deception and came up with something I just couldn't ignore. It's time to start taking this sensitivity thing seriously, my body seemed to be saying, and start taking care of yourself.

Along with the strange fruit and vegetable allergy, I also have low blood sugar or hypoglycaemia. If I eat too much sugar I'll get a headache and if I don't eat often enough I'll start acting like a drunk person on a weekend binge. Eventually I'll pass out and fall into a coma. I need to eat small, healthy meals every three hours to keep my blood sugar levels up and avoid raw sugar and processed foods. I try to see it as Nature's way of keeping me healthy.

After my doctor diagnoses me with hypoglycaemia, I go to see a dietician. She suggests some healthy snacks. How about carrot and celery sticks with peanut butter? she says. Or an apple and some almonds? Oh, dear.

I also experienced the physical effects of stress when I was working in a department store for a few months. I should have realized that the retail environment is probably the worst possible place for a highly sensitive person to be, let alone work in. But as usual, I was going to find that out the hard way. I was working in the jewellery department, showing pretty necklaces and matching earrings to ladies who were treating themselves to a night out.

And then came Christmas. Everyone seemed to be buying jewellery for their mother, sister, wife or girlfriend and quite often for themselves. If it wasn't the noise of the canned Christmas music blaring overhead, or the flashing festive lights, it was the crowds of eager and exhausted shoppers pushing their way to the front of the counter that overwhelmed me.

In a few weeks, I became so saturated with every kind of sensory and emotional stimulation that I developed TMJ, temporomandibular joint disorder. This joint connects your jaw to your skull and lets you move your jaw up and down. Working as a shop girl at Christmas had been so stressful for me that I was clenching my jaw during the day and grinding my teeth at night. Consequently, my jaw was sore, I couldn't open my mouth, it hurt to chew and I had to wear a night guard when I went to bed to protect my teeth. Clearly, retail work and sensitivity don't mix.

While my sensitivity does mean that I have to bring a suitcase of snacks to work every day and I can't visit a store without earplugs, I've got used to it. I can still enjoy the sweet smell of apples and pears and I've discovered the modern miracle of microwavable mashed potatoes. I can manage perfectly well, as long as I'm not too cold and it's not too crowded, I've had a protein snack in the last 45 minutes and I haven't been within five miles of any fruit-bearing alder trees. No problem.

Making sense of sensitivity

Highly sensitive people are particularly vulnerable to the effects of stress. We are constantly absorbing information from our environment as well as picking up tension and emotion from other people, which creates a state of constant over-arousal. While non-HSPs might be able to laugh about minor car trouble and accept a sudden change of plans due to a sick child, highly sensitive people feel the stress of those events more intensely. Some people enjoy the excitement of endless text messages and emails and invitations, but that rattles an HSP's nerves. When there is more than one stressor in one day, or on an ongoing basis, the stress is often more than we can handle. Stress takes a toll on both our sensitive nervous system and our immune system and it can affect us not only emotionally but physically.

Research (Benham 2006) shows that sensory processing sensitivity is associated with stress symptoms of ill health. Sensitive people are prone to developing allergies and sensitivities to certain foods, and to environmental and chemical agents. Some highly sensitive people are also vulnerable to blood sugar disorders, migraines and headaches, fibromyalgia and chronic fatigue, intense PMS symptoms, skin problems like eczema, hives and cold sores, insomnia, asthma, colds, flu and infections.

Stress triggers a 'fight-or-flight' response in your body, which is an instinctive way of trying to cope with perceived danger by fighting it or running away. To prepare for these reactions, your body releases stress hormones, such as adrenaline and cortisol, to boost your blood sugar levels and blood fats (triglycerides) to give you energy to fight or run. But we generally don't fight or run in the face of modern-day stress. Instead of releasing all that energy and those stress hormones through exercise, they remain in the body where, over the long term, they can create harmful conditions. Your muscles and joints become fatigued and inflammation develops. Your immune support diminishes and the symptoms of stress begin to appear (Aronson 2009).

Absorbing information is tiring. For highly sensitive people, the constant state of being overwhelmed and the stress that follows it is exhausting. When we experience a particularly overwhelming emotional or sensory experience, we need a lot of downtime to recover. The physical effects of stress take a toll on your energy levels, which can also leave you feeling anxious and depressed, which in turn can lower your self-esteem.

Sensitivity to pain

Highly sensitive people don't just feel emotions intensely. We also tend to feel physical sensations more acutely than others. According to Elaine Aron (2012b), having a highly sensitive nervous system means that some of us can feel more pain than other people do. We might need more anaesthetic at the dentist, for example, or in my case, enough to choke a horse. We might faint when a doctor takes blood or injects a needle. We tend to have a hard time with medical professionals in general, since their clinical approach can lead them to disregard our emotional needs, assume it's 'all in our minds' and question the intensity of our physical and emotional reactions.

Part of the problem for HSPs is convincing others that our feelings our real. Many healthcare practitioners are unfortunately unaware of high sensitivity and view our complaints about pain as childish whining. If it works for most people, they seem to say, it should work for you. But all too often, it doesn't. We're not like other people. And our pain is real.

Reactions to medications

Highly sensitive people also tend to react differently from non-HSPs to medications and treatments, says Aron (2012b). Sometimes we need more, sometimes less and sometimes it doesn't work at all. We can have bad or unusual reactions. So we need treatment that is individualized, precise and updated as our condition changes.

Many highly sensitive people are also very sensitive to the effects of caffeine, although I'm strangely unaffected by it. But a teaspoon of cough medicine will send me into a psychedelic spin that lasts for days.

Everyone is different and reacts differently to medications. And while highly sensitive people share a set of common traits, we all vary in our responses and the types of things we're sensitive to. What matters is finding out what affects you.

Sleep (aka not sleeping)

The constant process of absorbing information and emotions means that highly sensitive people need more rest, downtime and sleep than other people. At the same time, our sleep is often disturbed because we're so busy thinking and processing all that information. Despite our exhaustion, we often find we cannot fall asleep, or we wake up early and feel tired the next day. Consequently, our bodies are less equipped to cope with the next onslaught of stimulation we inevitably experience and we can quickly become burned out, sick, depressed and/or anxious. Lack of sleep also tends to make us feel more sensitive, so every day without sleep can become a struggle for survival.

Sleeping has always been difficult for me. I often wake up early as my mind swirls with thoughts, worries and strange dreams. I'm also highly sensitive to noise, temperature and light, so any whisper of sound from a ticking clock or a singing bird, a pinpoint of light from the rising sun, or a change in temperature will wake me up.

Finding ways to sleep better is an ongoing project, but I've become an expert at what doctors call good sleep hygiene. I have an evening routine that means I don't watch anything exciting or scary after 7 p.m., including the news. I drink chamomile and valerian tea. I read and listen to classical music. My bedroom is a highly sensitive oasis. Actually, it's more like an underground bunker – cool, dark and silent. I have a pillowtop mattress and 700 thread count Egyptian cotton sheets, hypoallergenic pillows, a lavender infuser, a blackout blind, blackout curtains, and earplugs. It may sound excessive, but you've got to look after your sensitive mind and body.

Emotions and your body

Some researchers, like scientist Bruce Lipton (2007), believe that the kind of physical response you have to a situation is a reflection of your emotional condition. In other words, your emotional state can lead to profound and correlated changes in the body. So feelings like resentment and bitterness can cause pain and inflammation, and an inflexible attitude can create stiff joints. Repressed hurt feelings can present themselves as arthritis, while deep hatred, guilt or grief can eat away at you like cancer. Back pain may be an indication of feeling lack of emotional support. Eye problems can suggest there is something you are not seeing clearly. A stiff jaw can indicate a lack of expression. Negative feelings such as shame, guilt, fear, anxiety, anger and hate will weaken your body, while positive emotions such as joy, love, understanding, forgiveness, acceptance and trust will strengthen it.

Your thoughts, emotions and your body work together and affect one another so when you experience physical symptoms, they can be an indication that you are experiencing stress.

One example of this in my own life was when my father died. In 2014, he was diagnosed with stage four inoperable pancreatic cancer. I was living in England and my father was living in Canada, so I was too far away to visit once he was diagnosed. But I was a stressed-out, nervous wreck. Despite the geographical distance, my dad and I were very close. I inherited my high sensitivity from him, along with many other wonderful qualities. Then one night, six weeks later, I got a phone call from my mother and I flew out to Canada the next day. Two days after that he passed away.

When I returned to England to go back to work, I noticed a strange rash on the back of my right hand. I'd never had anything like it before. It was red but then it turned into the shape of a heart. I had a perfect red heart on my hand that looked as if it had been tattooed there. At first, I was terrified that I had picked up some kind of infection. But then I felt that it was an expression of my feelings for my father. I had been crying and talking with my family and writing about my feelings, but it seemed that this wasn't enough, as if my feelings were too big and too powerful to be expressed in any traditional way. I was almost literally wearing my heart on my sleeve. The heart lasted for a couple of weeks and then it began to fade. I didn't want it to go. I wanted to keep this heart on my hand, this physical evidence of my love for my dad. It seemed like such a very highly sensitive way to express my feelings.

What I learned

Living in the world as a highly sensitive person means that everything around you is going to affect you and create greater stress on your emotions and your body than it will for other people. Consequently, finding ways to try to avoid becoming overstimulated or stressed and to decrease our susceptibility to illness is essential for our health and happiness. Here are a few things I've learned about how to cope.

1 **Listen to your body.** If you're a conscientious, hard-working, reliable and committed person, you're going to tend to keep going no matter what is going on. It can be hard to tell how stressed you really are or how your environment is affecting you, especially if you've spent your life ignoring or suppressing your sensitivity and your feelings. Many of us feel that we just need to soldier on, going to work, looking after our families, and putting ourselves last. But this creates an environment for illness. So it's important to listen to what your body is telling you. If you get a cold or the flu, you're probably run down and need to take it easy. Headaches, fatigue, skin problems and other physical ailments are all signs that you're overwhelmed and stressed. It's important not to ignore what your body is telling you and to start taking care of your sensitive self.

2 **Take some quiet time.** Highly sensitive people need a lot of rest. We need time on our own to rest physically from the overstimulation of living in a non-HSP world, but also to relax our minds. Under the pressure of living in a non-HSP society, we may push ourselves to get out there, believing that if we try harder, do more, act like everyone else, we'll finally find acceptance. But working, engaging with the world, participating in activities, trying to meet everyone's demands and expectations and generally rushing around will only lead to exhaustion and illness. Rest time is not a luxury. It's not laziness or a sign of weakness. It's as essential to an HSP as food and water.

Resting for highly sensitive people may not look the same as it does for others. Spending time with loved ones can still be draining. We need time alone so that we can think and process, and express ourselves creatively. Spend time doing things that increase your sense of flow, which is complete absorption in what you're doing, instead of worrying, which increases anxiety and stress. I think highly sensitive people are naturally good at creating a state of flow because we tend to live in the moment, intently focused on whatever we're doing. Sometimes we need a project we can throw our energy and compassion into. And sometimes we need to just stop thinking and listen to music, close our eyes, stare out of the window or go for a walk in nature.

3 **Get enough sleep.** Without sufficient sleep, our bodies don't get the chance to heal, repair themselves and restore us for another day. Stress is exhausting, so we need sleep to recuperate. When we don't get enough sleep, we feel tired, irritable and become vulnerable to more stress, creating a perpetual cycle that inevitably leads to ill health.

Highly sensitive people often need more sleep than other people, so don't be afraid to tell people what you need. That might include starting your bedtime routine at nine o'clock so that you have enough time to wind down. If you're staying overnight somewhere, ask for your own room or a room away from elevators and street noise. Do whatever you need to do to make it a quiet, comforting sanctuary.

4 **Listen to music.** Music can be a great way to relax. I find classical music really relaxing. I also love listening to movie soundtracks, perhaps because they're so emotionally evocative. Opera can make me cry. Jazz and blues make me feel deeply connected to my soul.

High sensitivity can so often seem like such a challenging condition that we forget that our sensitive senses can also enjoy positive sensory experiences. Listening to certain kinds of music can make me enter a state of such bliss that it makes me feel lucky to be so sensitive.

5 **Tell doctors and dentists you're highly sensitive.** Forget about trying to act tough. But don't succumb to feeling like a victim. Be proactive and tell people what you need. Even if your healthcare providers don't know what sensitivity is, tell them you're more sensitive to pain. I've done this with my dentist and, while she looked worried that I was going to burst into tears, she kindly asked me if I was okay throughout the procedure, to raise

my hand if I felt uncomfortable and told me what was going to happen before she started. And it helped. I was okay. She seemed relieved that I didn't turn out to be an emotional wreck. And her compassion made all the difference. You need to ask for what you need. She treated me like a sensitive person and that's just what my sensitive mind and body needed.

6 **Exercise.** Studies (Salmon 2001) show that physical activity helps alleviate anxiety, depression and sensitivity to stress. Exercise is particularly important for highly sensitive people because we absorb so much stimulation; we need an outlet for all that energy. Our ancestors burned off stress through their fight-or-flight reactions, but today we tend to simply sit and worry, which creates more stress and makes the body vulnerable to physical problems, illness and a weakened immune system.

Highly sensitive people also tend to be introverted and intro-spective thinkers. Much of our lives is lived internally, in our minds and imagination, and often in occupations that are office based. Physical activity helps to create a balance between the physical and the mental and offers us an opportunity to connect our minds with our bodies. In this way, we can understand ourselves as a whole even better, knowing that the way we think and feel affects us physically and that movement can provide us with strength, resilience, flexibility and relaxation for both the mind and the body.

I like to take long walks in the countryside whenever I can. For me, the combination of solitude, exercise and the peace and quiet of the natural world is a tonic for the mind, body and spirit. I feel relaxed and rejuvenated, and more in touch with my thoughts, feelings and my body. Running offers me the same thing. I run because I enjoy it. When I get a rhythm going, I get a 'runner's high', caused by the release of a number of brain chemicals, including endorphins. It elevates my mood, causing a feeling of euphoria mixed with decreased anxiety and suppression of pain. When I run, I can forget about everything and just focus on the moment and the beauty of the world around me. It's like a kind of meditation. The whole point of meditation is not to be a great meditator, but to let go of the worries and the stress that are preventing you from appreciating and enjoying the moment you're living.

You don't have to take up running to reap the rewards of exercise. To make it an enjoyable and stress-relieving activity, find something that you enjoy doing, whether it's aerobics, tennis, swimming or walking. For some people, running helps to burn off all that nervous energy we absorb. But others may find that calming exercises such as yoga, tai chi or gardening are more effective.

7 **Adopt a healthy diet.** If you have sensitivities or allergies to certain foods, talk to a dietician about how to create a healthy diet. In some cases, eliminating allergy triggers and then slowly reintroducing them can help your body to overcome its reaction to them. At the same time, a healthy diet will help highly sensitive people to have more energy, feel less depleted and enable their bodies to acquire the fuel and nutrients they need to cope with stress and avoid illness. Because highly sensitive people often have a more sensitive body, it's best to avoid processed foods and eat plenty of fresh fruit and vegetables. Try some new recipes and see how you can use your creativity in the kitchen to conjure up some delicious, nutritious meals.

8 **Adopt a healthy lifestyle.** Clear out anything in your life that causes you stress. Watching the news at night, for example, can be overly stimulating and anxiety-producing for HSPs, and consequently interfere with our ability to sleep. Try reducing your exposure to information and technology, which can overload anyone's mind. Take some time away from the computer, the phone and the TV and give yourself time to just relax. Clearing away the clutter in your home can also help. You might also need to let go of activities, clubs, jobs, and even people in your life who are causing you stress. Think of how each one of these makes you feel – if you feel rattled, anxious, flustered, worried, depressed, angry, frustrated, unhappy or unwell when you're around them, it may be time to let them go.

Highly sensitive people need to live in a positive, compassionate, and healthy environment to thrive. We need plenty of mental stimulation and minimal environmental stimulation. It may not be what other people need. But it's okay to assert your need for peace and quiet, and to live a highly sensitive life. Your health, happiness and your sensitive self depend on it.

4

Emotionality

'The best and most beautiful things in the world cannot be seen or even touched. They must be felt with the heart.'

Helen Keller

I'm 27 and living in Vancouver's Kitsilano neighbourhood, near the edge of English Bay. It's a Friday night and I'm going out to the movies with my friend Kirsten. She's also a highly sensitive person and I feel lucky to have found someone else like me. We met at work, when I was working in editorial and she was a graphic designer in the art department. Together, we visited her parents' cottage on Bowen Island and talked about music, art, writing and emotions and I felt like I'd found a soulmate.

That evening, we decide to see the film *Life is Beautiful*. It's about one family's experience of the Holocaust, but I didn't know that when we bought the tickets. I just liked the title.

Kirsten and I planned to go for coffee after the film, but when we walk out of the theatre into the cool night, lit up by street-lights and neon signs, we quickly abandon those plans. I sit silently in her car as she drives through the dark streets to take me home. Neither of us speak a word.

I open my front door, and as soon as I'm inside, I fall to my knees and sob uncontrollably for an hour. I can't contain it. I can't stop it. I can't bear the horrendous experiences that people went through. It feels almost as if I have been there in person, a silent and helpless witness to this massacre. It was such a graphic portrayal of what happened to people under the Nazi regime. But there was so much there that was about love and beauty and appreciating life. I found both of these equally moving and overwhelming. I'm sure Kirsten feels it the same way.

When another friend recommended *Schindler's List*, I knew I wasn't going to watch it. Not because I don't care, but because I care so much it hurts.

Making sense of sensitivity

Many people have told me I overreact. 'It's only a movie,' they say. 'Why are you making such a big deal out of it?' 'Just relax.' 'What's your problem?' Someone even asked me once if I needed medication, as if empathy and compassion and emotion were an illness. Many non-HSPs think that I have a problem, a weakness, a defect that needs fixing. They don't understand that I just feel things more intensely. But like most sensitive people, I have heard these kinds of comments many times, so I've learned to keep my feelings inside until I'm somewhere safe, where I can let it all out.

It's not just movies and television that upset me. I also cry when other people are upset. I'm not only aware of what they're feeling, I can feel it myself. I absorb their emotions. I also cry when I'm frustrated or angry. I cry in response to stress. I cry at toilet paper commercials. The digital age hasn't made it any easier. Even non-HSPs can attest to the frantic, frazzled pace of life these days and the endless demands that technology has placed on us. The constant beeping of electronic devices alone is enough to reduce me to tears. Let's just say I buy tissues in bulk.

Any situation or event that suggests the faintest possibility of anger, violence, threat, danger, negativity, noise, commotion, anguish, sorrow or discomfort gets crossed off my list. I try to avoid them, but that's not always possible. Consequently, that means everyday life can be rather stressful, so I try to do what makes me feel calm and peaceful, rather than being in the centre of things. But that's okay with me. I don't need a lot of stimulation or a lot of people to be happy. Some people need roller coasters and horror movies to feel anything. I need much less stimulation than that. A river, a book and Bach are thrilling enough for me.

But it's not just violence or sad experiences that elicit a strong emotional response in highly sensitive people. We also feel passionately about positive things. Any good news, whether it's for me or someone I care about, has me in tears. Any positive experience is intensely joyful and exhilarating – so much so that I wish I could give it to others. For example, I went to a New Year's Eve dance recently and everyone in the room spontaneously started doing the conga. No way, I said to my friend. There's no way I'm getting involved in that. I started making my way to a dark corner of the room, away from all the commotion, when a hand reached out and pulled me in. Suddenly I was doing the conga! I thought it was going to be a nightmare, but there was so much joy and happiness in the room, that I was laughing until tears ran down my face. The happiness felt so good, I was just euphoric. People started wondering why I was so jubilant, but I couldn't explain it. I just felt lucky that I was able to feel it.

Studies by Jagiellowicz et al. (2011) found that HSPs react more intensely to positive images than non-HSPs, especially if they had a good childhood. The results appeared in areas of the brain associated with strong emotions, but also in areas of thinking and perceiving.

My feelings are big and intense. It's like the emotional part of me is twice the size of everyone else's. And yet I'm not a showy person. I'm pretty quiet and don't talk much, unless I have something important to say. I don't like to be the centre of attention. I just think of myself as passionate.

I don't think feeling emotions is the enemy. *Not* feeling anything is. Stumbling through life like an automaton is what drags us down and holds us back. I am lucky to be able to feel so much. If that means I'm in tears of joy or crying over a commercial, it's worth it because I know I have experienced life fully. I'm living life passionately, not superficially. I'm not pretending or faking anything. Every day is alive.

But the constant intensity of our feelings can be overwhelming both for ourselves and for others and most sensitive people struggle to cope with them on a daily basis. We absorb more, we process more and so we feel more, and then we process those feelings. Unfortunately, non-HSPs may believe that we're volatile, hysterical, irrational and out of control. There seems to be a common misconception that HSPs are emotional ticking time bombs, ready to explode with rage or tears at the slightest provocation. But what research has shown is that highly sensitive people simply have brains that feel more and react more to both positive and negative experiences.

Another study (Brindle et al. 2015) found that highly sensitive people are more aware of their emotions, and we also have more negative ones, such as depression, anxiety and feeling very stressed, which isn't surprising considering the overstimulation and criticism we often have to deal with. The study suggests that repeatedly feeling overwhelmed affects our ability to accept our emotional states and our confidence that we can control them. Consequently, this can lead to further negative feelings.

Many highly sensitive people have had so many negative reactions to their emotional natures from others that they find it hard to know how to cope. The general lack of acceptance of sensitive people often causes an HSP to withdraw and feel afraid, insecure, confused and ashamed. It's no wonder we have a hard time dealing with our feelings or feeling good about who we are.

Emotional regulation is the way we deal with our feelings. According to Elaine Aron (2015), it's the way we 'consciously or unconsciously influence what emotions we have, when we have them, and how we experience and express them'. Since highly sensitive people feel emotions more intensely and consequently are more prone to negative feelings like depression and anxiety and to feeling stressed, emotional regulation is an important skill to learn.

What I learned

What I've learned is that I cannot change my emotional nature or the intensity of my feelings, but I can manage them and so can you. It takes practice and the belief that you are all right, just the way you are, and that your needs matter.

1 **Breathe**. When you're feeling afraid or anxious (another word for fear), your mind and body go into 'fight-or-flight' mode, which prepares you to either run away or fight. Your heart rate goes up, and blood starts rushing away from your brain and into your muscles, making it harder to think. It's a normal, instinctive reaction to what we perceive as a danger or threat. This basic instinct evolved to help protect us from things like stampedes of

wildebeests and men with spears. But it is still triggered when we *believe* something is a danger or a threat to us, such as speaking in public, watching a horror film or, in my case, going grocery shopping. *Acting* on this instinct can quickly get you into trouble because your mind is focused on survival rather than on common sense. In other words, you cannot think clearly or act rationally when you're upset.

When you feel anxious, stop. Don't do anything – unless you're being chased by a swarm of killer bees, in which case you should run away. But just like any dangerous situation, emotions are temporary. Whatever you're feeling is not an expression of who you are. It will pass. While you're waiting, take a few long, slow, deep breaths. According to the American Institute of Stress (2012), breathing is the best way to relax. It changes your physical and emotional response to stress by lowering your heart rate and blood pressure, and relaxing your muscles. It raises the level of hormones that make you feel good, such as oxytocin and dopamine, and lowers cortisol, the hormone released by stress. Increased circulation increases blood supply to the brain and the increase in oxygen helps you to think more clearly.

Breathing also makes you more aware of your body. By simply focusing on breathing in and breathing out, your attention becomes centred on your body instead of the anxious thoughts in your mind.

Once you feel calm again, you can *choose* how you want to respond to the situation. Intense emotions are like intense people. You don't have to interact with them. Just take a step back, take a deep breath and give yourself the time you need to decide what you want to do next.

2 **Let it out.** We're all encouraged to hide our feelings and 'tough it out' or 'keep a stiff upper lip'. Whether you're male or female, not showing your feelings is somehow seen as a sign of strength. Let me tell you the truth – it isn't. It's a sign that you're good at hiding your feelings. And the more you hide them, the more they will eat away at you. They don't just go away. It's like shoving something in the closet and pretending it's not there. And because you're hiding it, you keep thinking about it, and worrying that someone will find it and expose you and all your secrets. That's what keeps you locked in the past and unable to

get over difficult experiences. And that's what keeps you feeling sad, frustrated, depressed, anxious and unhappy.

Expressing my feelings in a safe, quiet place is what has helped me to get over many difficult circumstances. I cry, write in my journal, walk in the woods and talk to someone I trust. And then I do it some more, and then some more until I have nothing left to say and no more tears to shed. Having such depth of feelings forces highly sensitive people to be aware of them and to deal with them on a daily basis. We can't ignore them. So we need to face them head on. Figure out what you're feeling and express it. I see this as a great strength. Expressing my feelings is the best way I know of clearing out the clutter of the past, and freeing me to move on unencumbered and happy.

3 **Use your emotional intelligence.** I believe one of the benefits of being highly sensitive is our unique combination of self-awareness, empathy and emotionality, which leads us to being emotionally intelligent. Psychologist Daniel Goleman, author of *Emotional Intelligence* (1995) developed the idea that emotional intelligence is the ability to recognize your own and other people's emotions and to use emotions to guide your thinking and behaviour.

Research by Sunil and Rooprai (2009) shows that high emotional intelligence is a significant factor in helping people manage stress and anxiety. It also helps us to avoid sources of stress and to deal effectively with the level of emotional arousal we experience. Importantly, emotional intelligence is a skill that can be learned.

It's a great asset to be able to understand others on an emotional level and to use that knowledge to help people understand themselves. You may feel overwhelmed by your emotions, but when you realize that they are there to help you understand yourself, you can gain greater insight into your own identity. HSPs are capable of enormous emotional intelligence – we just need the confidence to know that big feelings are not a weakness, but a strength.

4 **Do things you enjoy.** Doing what you like to do is a key part of learning to manage your emotions because it builds confidence. When you spend time doing things you enjoy, your body, mind and emotions relax and recharge. This is how you can stop feeling like a swingball, bounced around from one stressful experience to

another and always *reacting* instead of *acting*, always struggling to cope.

It doesn't matter what it is, as long as you enjoy it. For highly sensitive people, that often includes activities that aren't what most people call 'fun,' such as going shopping or spending the day at an amusement park. For us, it may be quieter outings, like a walk in nature or spending time with animals, reading, listening to music, or a creative activity, like painting, drawing, writing or dancing. The important thing is to not let anyone talk you out of what you enjoy. Just do it.

Choosing how to spend your free time by doing things you like also gives you a sense of empowerment and a feeling of freedom. The more you do them, the better you get. It becomes easier and more fun and you feel more relaxed and happy. And you are spending time doing things that are true to who you really are. And that's what will give you confidence. When you have confidence, you can manage your emotions and responses better because you trust that you can. You are in control of your own life. When you have confidence, you can do anything.

5 **Learn about yourself.** Many highly sensitive people have spent their lives listening to negative remarks and criticisms about who they are. Sometimes people mean well and say things because they want to help. Unfortunately, many people will try to tell you who you are and what you should do and not do because they think they know you. But when people say disparaging things about you it's because they don't know who you really are. They're actually talking about themselves, not you. People often act out of their own fears and try to put you down to make themselves feel better. But if you don't know who you really are, you'll believe whatever they say.

In a study of American college students, researchers (Shin et al. 2016) revealed that a clear self-concept significantly predicted a sense of meaning in life. When you learn about yourself and your natural traits, you know who you really are and what you need to be happy. You can feel confident because everything about you is clear and life becomes more meaningful. And then you can ignore the critical remarks, secure in the knowledge that you know the truth about who you are and that your life has meaning, no matter what anyone says.

5

Low self-esteem

'Always be a first-rate version of yourself, instead of a second-rate version of someone else.'

Judy Garland

I'm 12 years old when I move with my family from London, Ontario, to Burlington, a small suburban city on the commuter line between Hamilton and Toronto. We moved several times before, first from England to Ontario, where we lived in a couple of different neighbourhoods. All of these places were nice, safe, middle-class suburban areas where my sister and I could ride our bikes down the street and enjoy barbecues with our neighbours. But I am afraid to do most things on my own.

I can't walk to the local corner store by myself. I feel overwhelmed by the outside world, and overstimulated by the noise on the streets, the sound of cars roaring down the road, the sharp peaks of people talking, the shouts of boys playing soccer, dogs barking, babies crying. We live on a fairly quiet street, but it doesn't take much to rattle my sensitive nervous system. I'm constantly absorbing and processing. Most of the time, I just feel nervous, partly because I'm always overstimulated and partly because everyone's lack of understanding of my sensitivity makes me question my own self-worth.

I think my parents and teachers are worried that I'm too quiet and too shy and that with a little push, I will get over it. I think their idea is that spending lots of time on my own and doing strange things like sitting in my room for hours writing poetry is *causing* me to be shy and insecure and sensitive. If I can get out there and mingle with the other kids, I will soon make lots of boisterous friends and be happy as a clam. I can understand their rationale. At this point, no one has even heard of high sensitivity. I know they're trying to do the right thing. They just want me to be happy. But the more they push and encourage me to be like everyone else, to be more outgoing and assertive, the more I feel that there is something wrong with me.

Unfortunately, most of the activities at school seem to cater to non-HSP extraverts. They focus on group activities, lots of participation and not a lot of time for quiet reflection. I struggle to keep up with the games and the noise. It just doesn't feel much fun to me. My mind is too busy thinking, processing, imagining, and creating to be able to focus on the activity going on around me. So I withdraw even further.

At lunchtime, I sneak away to the far corner of the school property to read or take a walk or just sit and think on my own, but people ask me what's wrong and so I assume there must be something wrong with me. When I comment on the noise, the light, the temperature, the crowds, I'm told I should stop complaining. Nobody else is bothered by the things that bother me. Nobody else is complaining. So it makes sense, to my parents, my teachers, my Brownie leaders, and to me, that the problem isn't the cold or the lights or the noise or the throbbing energy of a roomful of people. The problem is me.

Consequently, I try to be like everyone else. I try to stop complaining, stop being so picky and stop being so sensitive. Like most children, I just want to fit in. I just want to belong. I know I feel different, but I look like everyone else. It's not like having a broken arm. People will feel compassion for you if you're wearing a cast. They can understand your struggles if you're in a wheelchair. But if not, they assume you're just lazy, stupid, petulant, demanding, selfish, shy or weak.

Needless to say, my attempt to fit in and 'overcome' my sensitivity doesn't work. In fact, it makes me feel worse because I keep failing. I am not very good at being a non-sensitive person. I don't enjoy team sports. I feel overwhelmed by group discussions. I can't bear noise. So my self-esteem sinks even further.

Making sense of sensitivity

Low self-esteem doesn't originate from one experience. It's a long, slow, drip-feed of repeated criticisms and negative beliefs that wear away your sense of self-worth like raindrops on a stone. Eventually, there's an empty space in your middle where something solid should be, but it happens so gradually and with such familiarity, you don't even know it's happening. You can't imagine any other way of being or how to fill that emptiness inside you.

Low self-esteem can take on many forms. It can reveal itself overtly as self-loathing or lack of assertiveness. It can affect our relationships, as we tend to get involved with people who treat us as badly as we believe we deserve or the way we're used to being treated. It can also create negative attitudes and behaviours such as defensiveness, lack of trust, perfectionism, materialism or exhibiting a controlling, people-pleasing or self-sabotaging personality. I've written more about these behaviours in my book *Overcoming Low Self-Esteem with Mindfulness*.

Many people think high sensitivity and low self-esteem are the same thing, but they're not. Low self-esteem is a way of thinking about yourself as inadequate, unacceptable, unworthy, unlovable and/or incompetent. This is not an inherent characteristic of high sensitivity.

But for highly sensitive people, low self-esteem is a common result of the criticism and lack of understanding that others have about HSPs. We learn early on that our way of seeing and experiencing the world is unusual and unacceptable, something we need to change. But we can't change any more than a horse can stop startling at a sudden noise or a dog can stop trembling during a thunderstorm. We believe that there's something wrong with us, that we've failed in some way, and so we begin to feel bad about ourselves. This is what leads to low self-esteem – the feeling that the person you are just isn't good enough.

High sensitivity is not the same thing as shyness either. While high sensitivity is the sense of feeling *overwhelmed* by sensory, emotional and social experiences, shyness is the *fear* of social interactions. Shy people avoid social situations because they are afraid that they will be rejected. Highly sensitive people avoid social situations because we find them exhausting. We'd have more fun spending time alone or with one or two other people. As a child, I was highly sensitive and shy and an introvert. It's amazing I ever got out of the house.

Highly sensitive people are also more vulnerable to developing low self-esteem because we tend to absorb and internalize negative messages and experiences so deeply. We soak up other people's feelings and energy like a sponge, which means all the irritation, disdain, contempt and anger flying around gets into our bloodstream and becomes lodged, somewhere, deep inside in our hearts and minds where we come to believe it's part of who we are.

Sensitivity, depression and anxiety

Because highly sensitive people absorb so much stimulation from our environment and consequently feel overwhelmed, we are more susceptible to feelings of anxiety. A study by Montag et al. (2008) showed that people with a more sensitive 'startle' reflex, that is, highly sensitive people, are more susceptible to anxiety disorders because specific variations in the gene that regulates dopamine makes it harder for us to ignore emotional arousal.

After years of studying anxiety sufferers, anxiety expert Charles Linden (*Anxiety and Stress Relief Resources*) also revealed that all of the 130,000 study subjects shared a high level of creative intellect. People with greater sensory processing sensitivity have characteristics like openness to experience that can make us more prone to anxiety but also more creative.

Similarly, overstimulation can lead us to feeling depressed. But being highly sensitive does not mean you will develop depression or an anxiety disorder. It depends on your genes and your upbringing and how you learn to cope. According to Elaine Aron (1996), if you were brought up in an environment that supported your sensitivity, you're less likely to develop depression or anxiety because you feel good about who you are. If you had a difficult childhood, you're more likely to suffer from those conditions. Feeling anxious or depressed can in turn make you question yourself and your worth and lower your self-esteem.

But even if you do feel anxious or depressed, it's not necessarily something that needs to be 'fixed' unless it's becoming a problem for you or interfering with things like your work, relationships or health.

HSPs often feel anxious because of all the energy, emotion and information we're constantly absorbing. As I said earlier, highly sensitive people have gates with very big holes in them, which allow a lot of stimulating information to come rushing into our internal world. That's part of what makes us creative and capable of seeing possibilities, but it also means we accumulate a lot of information and emotion. And that stuff needs somewhere to go or else our personal space is bursting. This feeling that it's all too much and you've become saturated like a wet sponge is what can make us feel anxious and jittery. It's an energy overload combined with a fear that we won't be able to survive.

The highly sensitive man

High sensitivity is an inherited trait, and I inherited mine from my father. He couldn't stand a lot of noises either. For him, it was a bird that was a particular source of stress. This bird liked to sit in the trees in my parents' garden and sing. Except it wasn't singing. It was a loud, high-pitched trill. It was annoying to me, but for my dad it was torture. He tried everything he could to deal with it – wearing noise-cancelling headphones, firing at it with the garden hose spray gun, swearing at it and threatening it. He became convinced that the bird was tormenting him on purpose. It sounds funny that a man felt bullied by a bird, but it was unbearable for him. Sometimes, he had to stop gardening and come inside because he couldn't stand it anymore. Once I saw him rushing in from the garden cursing under his breath, his eyes full of tears.

Being male and highly sensitive can be a challenge. Men are taught from a young age that asking for help and showing their feelings are signs of weakness, so they learn to suppress any negative emotion except anger. The result, says HSP researcher Dr Ted Zeff, author of the book *The Strong, Sensitive Boy*, is that many men suffer in silence. And this repression of their true feelings can have dire consequences for their relationships, career and health.

Highly sensitive men often bury their feelings in an attempt to conform to social pressure and as a way of dealing with the emotions they may not understand or know how to deal with. By suppressing unpleasant feelings, such as fear, anxiety, worry and hurt, a man can find it easier to function. Unfortunately, human emotions are complex and interconnected, so if you bury one, you bury them all, including the positive ones, like happiness, enthusiasm and love. This strategy may make life easier for the highly sensitive man, but it also makes his life flat, cold and ultimately lonely. He can become emotionally distant from the people he cares about and who care about him, making it nearly impossible for him to receive the love and support he needs.

According to Elaine Aron (1996), high sensitivity appears in men and women in equal numbers. When a woman bursts into tears when she's overwhelmed, people tend to respond with compassion. When a highly sensitive man responds that way, he's treated with criticism and contempt. He is ostracized, rejected and humiliated. He's expected to hide his feelings, suck it up and soldier on. Showing feelings and acting with empathy and compassion are seen as feminine qualities and, in a boy, abnormal. None of these responses is helpful, and the negative way in which highly sensitive men and boys are perceived and treated can rip their self-confidence to shreds.

I've known several highly sensitive men, including my father, and despite the common belief that men have to be tough, I find their sensitivity very attractive. I love that they show their feelings and possess so much creativity. I love their warmth and gentleness. And of course, I love how much we have in common. As my dad and I learned about and accepted our sensitivity, it became one of the things that drew us closer together.

Unfortunately, many highly sensitive men struggle not only with revealing their sensitivity to the world, but also with accepting themselves. It's understandable why men who are sensitive would want to hide their sensitive traits so that they will be more accepted, by other men and by women. But the effort required to suppress your true nature can be exhausting and debilitating, so much so that you don't have the energy or focus to devote to anything or anyone else.

Sensitivity isn't something you choose. It's something you're born with, so you can't change it. Consequently, men can easily feel bad about themselves if they believe their sensitivity is a weakness and their self-esteem can continue to take hits throughout their lives.

The highly sensitive woman

In many ways, being highly sensitive is easier for women. There is a gender stereotype that accepts sensitivity in females. We think it's normal that women cry sometimes and show their feelings. And we are less likely to judge a woman negatively for becoming emotional.

Traditionally, women have been seen as gentle, emotional, fragile creatures who need to be protected from the harshness of the real world. And while this may seem like an approval of sensitivity in women, this view of course sees sensitivity as a weakness and overlooks the strengths and gifts that come with it. Just as men can be both sensitive and masculine, women can be sensitive and strong.

Another assumption about women continues to persist in our society, making it difficult for sensitive women to feel accepted for who they are. While men are often expected to be the strong, silent type, hiding their emotions and 'toughing it out' in every situation, women are frequently assumed to be the opposite – talkative, outgoing, gregarious people who love to socialize. Many people assume that all women have plenty of friends and love to spend time talking and being around other people. It's assumed that women need other women, and that being 'one of the girls' is essential to our survival and our identity. A woman on her own is suspect and often the subject of pity. There is a common perception that even if she chooses to be alone, there must be something wrong with her.

I once went into a pub on my own to have a quiet, reflective drink at the bar. I'd just been visiting my grandmother and I was worried that she was showing signs of dementia. I was far from home and I didn't feel like going back to my hotel room. But as soon as I walked in, everyone fell silent. I'm pretty sure it wasn't because of my stunning good looks. I sat at the bar, ordered a gin and tonic and expected I might get a bit of friendly banter from the bartender, or perhaps the people sitting next to me.

What I got instead was an unmistakable feeling of anxiety and nervousness from everyone around me. Being a highly sensitive person, of course, I could feel it intensely. And I knew that no one believed I was there just to relax, have a drink and think about things on my own. Apparently, women aren't supposed to be the strong, silent type.

Highly sensitive women have different needs and desires from non-HSP women. Because we can become overstimulated by too much activity, too much noise and too many people around us, we need a lot of downtime. We need time alone to think and reflect and to recharge our batteries. We need to spend time doing quiet things, like reading or walking in the woods or pursuing creative activities.

Similarly, highly sensitive women tend not to enjoy stereotypically 'female' activities like shopping or a day out at an amusement park with friends and the kids. It's just too overwhelming. Even the hectic pace of life as a modern parent can often feel like too much. There is so much emphasis on getting children involved in organized activities and developing their social skills that there isn't enough time for either parents or kids to get the quiet time they need. And learning how to play and work alone is important. Even little children need some time to just play without a schedule. It gives them a chance to relax and promotes their sense of identity, self-awareness, emotional development and creativity (Galanaki 2005). And highly sensitive parents need time to recharge as well.

The natural ability of a highly sensitive woman to be compassionate and empathetic also means that she can easily become a personal therapist to friends, colleagues and anyone who needs a helping hand. Because we can feel other people's emotions, we often take them on, along with the issues associated with them, as if they were our own. Highly sensitive people like to help others, and our well-developed listening skills and ability to put ourselves in someone else's shoes can seem like a life preserver to those in need. For highly sensitive women, however, it can be difficult to draw a line between offering help and throwing ourselves in at the deep end.

Unfortunately, some people will take advantage of our caring nature and keep taking while giving nothing back because they are so focused on their own needs. Others may assume that sensitive women who care about others don't need anything themselves. And we can indeed quickly become lured into believing that we don't need time or space for ourselves. Putting other people first is what many girls are raised to believe they must do and we grow up thinking that taking time for ourselves is just selfish. But giving too much to other people and not taking the quiet time we need only leaves us feeling exhausted and weakens our self-esteem, as we wonder why we feel so bad when we've given so much.

What I learned

Low self-esteem is not a characteristic of high sensitivity, but many highly sensitive people feel bad about themselves because of the lack of acceptance and understanding they've experienced regarding their sensitivity. Fortunately, low self-esteem can be undone and confidence can be learned. Here are a few things I've learned that have helped me to build my self-confidence and love who I am.

1 **Accept who you are.** I'm an introvert and I'm highly sensitive. Those are things that I can't change, although some studies (Dweck 2008) suggest that we can become more introverted or extraverted over time. Sensitivity can't change, and I don't want to change it. But I'm no longer shy and I now have pretty healthy self-esteem. I think I developed my self-confidence by understanding and accepting who I am and developing a strong sense of identity instead of trying to change it. That's how you realize that you have a special place in the world and that the world needs you the way you are. HSPs are very independent people and can't stand feeling trapped. Learning to identify and accept yourself is the first step on the road to freedom.

   If you're a highly sensitive man, recognizing and accepting yourself as highly sensitive is key. Despite what you may have been told, sensitivity is a strength, not a weakness. It means that you're creative, compassionate, empathetic and able to appreciate things that other people often miss. Being highly sensitive also means that you have a unique ability to understand and help others. Burying your feelings may feel easier. Talking about your emotions and your needs takes courage. But by accepting yourself and your powerful feelings, and learning to express them in a healthy way, you not only draw loving people towards you but you can also teach others how to cope, simply by being an example of sensitivity and strength.

2 **Change your beliefs.** It is the beliefs in our subconscious mind that often control our behaviours, actions, decisions and choices in life. You don't have to blame anyone for the way you are, but you do need to stop believing the negative talk in your head. It will only make you feel bad about yourself. Once you start thinking of yourself in a more positive way, your life will begin to change for the better.

The good thing about learned behaviour is that we can unlearn it. We may not have had any choice as children, but as an adult, you can choose to feel good about yourself. You can choose to live life the way you want to. You just have to believe you're worth the effort. I consciously tried to become aware of the thoughts in my mind that were holding me back and I made a conscious effort to change them. One effective way of doing this is questioning them. If you hear yourself thinking things like, 'I'm such an idiot', or 'I'll never make it', question it. Remember, these thoughts were probably put into your mind by someone else. They're not a part of you. Ask yourself, 'Am I really an idiot?' 'Is it really impossible for me to succeed?' and then find evidence to the contrary. You will.

3 **Get new information.** We often repeat the same behaviour while hoping for different results and get frustrated when things don't change. That's because we're using the same information that we've understood all our lives, information that may not be helpful or even correct. To break out of negative patterns, you need new information, which will give you a new way of looking at yourself and your situation. I've learned a lot of things from reading, but, most importantly, I've discovered fresh perspectives on things that I wouldn't have known otherwise. This can be so startling that I've experienced those moments when the light suddenly goes on in your head and you see what's really going on. That moment came for me when I read Elaine Aron's book. I recognized myself on every page. Finally, I could describe and explain how I felt, instead of believing that I was flawed. Suddenly, the way I felt and experienced the world made sense. It also happened when I read Iyanla Vanzant's excellent book

In the Meantime, which made me see how my perception of myself was holding me back.

Confidence doesn't come from living a perfect, easy life or having money, fame and success. It comes from the choices you make when you face adversity and from realizing that you can overcome hard times. When you believe that you deserve to be treated better than you are, you see those obstacles as speed bumps, not barriers, and you ride over them, driving yourself ever forward in the direction of your dreams.

4 **Connect.** In a way, I think feeling good about yourself as a highly sensitive person is like being a recovering alcoholic. It's not that highly sensitive people are addicted, but the comfort that comes from the understanding, compassion and acceptance of other people who are like us, in a group of like-minded people or a support organization, can give us the strength to start treating ourselves with love. I found that in Aron's book and I'm hoping you will find it here.

5 **Do what you love.** Do the things that make you feel happy, relaxed and fulfilled, and try to avoid the ones that make you feel anxious, stressed and unhappy. Pretty good advice for anyone, I'd say, but it's harder than it sounds. It means being aware of how you're feeling all the time. Fortunately, this is something highly sensitive people are good at. You may not have much choice about how much money you can spend, but you can choose how to spend your free time. Just because everyone is meeting up at the local bar every Friday night doesn't mean you have to. If you notice that you feel happier and calmer and more fulfilled spending your Saturday afternoons writing poetry or walking alone in the woods or watering your plants instead of going shopping with your friends, then do it.

What I discovered was that the more time I spent doing the things I liked to do, things that made me feel good, relaxed and mentally stimulated without sensory overload, the more I became a calmer, more confident person. For me, that meant writing, reading, learning, running, swimming, listening to music and taking long walks in nature whenever I could.

Many of us have the idea that doing what we want to do is selfish. It's not. Forget that idea. We all have responsibilities and we need to be considerate and caring towards other people, but we can spend our spare time in any way we like. And when you spend it in ways that fill your soul and allow you to express who you really are, you will start to realize that you have something to share with the world and that the world needs you to be who you are.

The more you practise being yourself, recognizing your individual talents and skills and positive qualities, the more you will begin to feel good and think positively about yourself. You'll also develop those skills and find fresh sources of pride and satisfaction that come from realizing you have unique abilities. When you fill yourself with confidence, you can give without fear because you know you don't need anyone else to boost your self-esteem. You can give that to yourself.

6 **Keep your relationships equal.** Our desire to help others is so strong that our relationships with others can easily become one-sided. In our friendships, romantic attachments and family associations, highly sensitive people often take on the role of counsellor, listening and offering sympathy to everyone around us. But in his book, *Emotional Vampires*, Albert Bernstein suggests it's important to avoid acting like a therapist to someone you care about. It's in your HSP wiring to want to help, but practising psychotherapy on someone will make them well and you sick. Being there for loved ones is important, but make sure they are there for you too.

7 **Avoid people with low self-esteem.** It's easy for highly sensitive people to become drawn to people who are suffering or need our help. We are highly empathic, meaning that we can easily feel other people's feelings, and we want to do something about them. But instead of you lifting them up, hurt people will often bring you down. Someone who has low self-esteem is like a drowning man and he's looking for a life preserver to cling to. Only someone who is standing on solid ground can give you what you need. A drowning person may not intend to use you. He or she may be a very nice person. They may want to be there for you and help you and love you, but they can't do it. They are too busy fighting for their own survival and looking for support, validation, approval and acceptance. What I learned about developing my self-esteem as a highly sensitive person is that the only life I need to rescue is mine.

6
Empathy

'Empathy is seeing with the eyes of another, listening with the ears of another, and feeling with the heart of another.'

Alfred Adler

I'm sitting cross-legged in front of a campfire that has gone out. We lit it the night before, and now, in the early morning of a cool day in August, three other little girls and I sit staring at the charred, black remains. I'm ten years old and this is our first day of Girl Guide camp, which is basically a dry patch of land in the middle of a field, somewhere on the outskirts of suburban London, Ontario.

I don't know whose idea it was for me to join the Girl Guides, but it seems like a pretty un-HSP thing to do, considering the large group activities, the games, the rules and the militaristic associations. To top it off, I'm not much of a camper. I have a difficult time sleeping on 700 thread-count Egyptian cotton sheets, let alone hard ground and cold tents. I also have the survival skills of a brick.

I was in the Brownies before the Guides, when I was about seven or eight. I think I wanted to join them because my best friend at the time was in the Brownies and her mum was one of the leaders. Her name was Mrs Gilmour, but at the Brownie meetings we called her Brown Owl. All the leaders were named after owls. I don't know why. Maybe it made them feel important.

At the Girl Guide camp, once we have set up our tents and our sleeping bags, we are given our first task – we have to go out into the woods, collect some sticks and use them to make a luggage rack. They will provide the string. Even as a child, I know this is a fairly unreasonable request, but I dutifully scurry off into the trees and come back with as many sticks and branches as my skinny little arms can carry, which is about three.

Two hours later, I have tied the three sticks together and am struggling to figure out how I am going to make this work. The Owls in charge tell us that we won't get any dinner until our camp racks are finished. I crouch in my damp tent, my hands trembling with the fear that I will go to bed hungry. Eventually, one of the Guide leaders sticks her head into my tent and looks at my efforts – my suitcase sitting on top of a pile of sticks. Never mind, she says, it's time for dinner. I guess I won't be getting a badge for luggage-rack making.

Dinner that night is sloppy joe on a bun, and we are told, once again, that we won't get any dessert until we have finished all our dinner. Unfortunately, they have given me enough sloppy joe to feed a lumberjack and a bun the size of my head. Trembling with fear of recrimination, I eat as much as I can and then press the remaining half of the bun into the sides of my plate. There, I think. They'll never see it now.

The next task is to make dessert. We're sitting in a circle and one of the leaders holds up a cardboard box and a roll of aluminium foil. Using these items, we have to make an oven and bake a cake in it. I think there might also be something to do with sunlight and matches as well, but I am too stunned to focus on the details. At this point, I'm beginning to wish I was back in the woods looking for sticks. Needless to say, my cardboard oven does not work but at least I haven't set any of my fellow Girl Guides on fire.

Later on, four of us are sitting around our little campfire again. One of the other girls is telling us how much she loves the Girl Guides and what a great time she's having at camp. She loves the outdoors and the games and making new friends. She's hoping to earn her Advanced Camper badge and maybe the Birdwatcher badge too, she says. And then she starts to cry.

'What's wrong?' says one of the other girls.

'I don't know,' she sobs, wiping her tears with her hand. She was drawing in the ashes with a stick and now her face is smeared with dirt. 'I've never been away from home before. I thought it would be fun.'

'It is fun. We're having fun, right?'

'Yes, I know, but,' she draws in a sharp breath, 'I just miss my mom.'

The other girls sit staring blankly at her, not knowing what to do or to say. But she keeps crying. And then I realize that I am crying too. And I know it isn't because I'm homesick. It's because she is. And I can feel it.

Making sense of sensitivity

In his 2009 book, *The Age of Empathy*, psychologist Frans de Waal suggested that empathy is linked to the brain's mirror neurons, which help us understand and mimic the behaviour of others. Listening to others' distress also releases oxytocin in the brain, the 'tend and befriend' chemical that's released when a mother bonds with her baby or when we have sex. Oxytocin causes us to reach out to others, care for them, and seek mutual support and nurturing.

Empathy is more than just recognizing what someone is feeling. It's putting yourself in someone else's shoes so you really know what it feels like to be in their situation. Everyone has the ability to feel empathy and most people do. That's why we put an arm around someone who's crying or offer reassuring words when they've had a bad day. But most of the time, we reserve these acts for people we know well, for family and friends. When it comes to strangers, it's harder to know what they're really going through and harder to show our compassion.

Many people struggle with finding enough empathy for others. They find it difficult to imagine what someone else might be feeling. But highly sensitive people struggle with having too much empathy. My problem is not trying to put myself into other people's shoes, but wedging myself back into my own. Social pressure to think of others first doesn't help. Our Brownie mantra was 'Think of others before you think of yourself'. I think the Brownies have a lot to answer for! I have spent so much time thinking of other people and their problems that my own shoes often felt foreign and unfamiliar to me. This is what can lead highly sensitive people to becoming people pleasers and giving too much.

Highly sensitive people experience empathy on a more intense level, like we do everything else. I'm not psychic, but I can often tell how someone is feeling just by being in the same room with them. They don't even have to say anything. I can feel it. It happens with people I know well and with complete strangers. The stronger their feelings, the more intensely I feel it. A study by Elaine Aron and her colleagues has revealed that this kind of empathy is more than just learned behaviour. Our HSP minds are built for empathy. The research (Acevedo et al. 2014) shows that highly sensitive people have greater activity in the brain regions associated with empathy, as well as awareness, information processing and action planning.

People often come to highly sensitive people with their problems because they can see we're empathic and good listeners and we genuinely care. But to be an 'empath' means that we're also absorbing the pain and suffering of others, which takes a toll on our own health and well-being.

Unfortunately, studies show that people who are most skilled at empathizing feel the cost of caring the most. In one study (Smith and Rose 2011), researchers found that people who can most easily put themselves in someone else's shoes, as an HSP can, are most likely to feel overwhelmed when they care for that person.

Another study (Schieman and Turner 2001) found that empathy is more likely to create symptoms of depression when people have lower self-esteem. Since highly sensitive people tend to be both empathic and often have low self-esteem, we're vulnerable to feeling overwhelmed, anxious and depressed as a consequence of caring.

What makes this additionally challenging is that we can be unsure whether the feelings we experience are our own or someone else's. I'm not just *aware* of how someone is feeling, I'm *feeling* it. I can find myself feeling sad, frustrated or angry without knowing why, until I realize that those feelings belong to someone else and I've simply soaked them up.

Because we feel more, we can also run the risk of giving more, and giving too much. The closer I am to someone emotionally, the more I absorb their feelings and want to do something about them. At times, this has left me feeling pressed under the weight of emotions I seem to have no control over, and exhausted from the effort of dealing with them.

We can become an extension of someone else rather than a separate person offering a helping hand, leading us to spend all our energy and resources trying to deal with someone else's feelings and problems instead of our own. This not only hurts us but it hurts the other person too because they're not learning from their own experiences. We're doing all the learning and experiencing for them.

Highly sensitive people feel different and experience the world differently because we are different. We were born this way and empathy is simply part of our wiring. In her book, *The Philosophical Baby*, psychologist Alison Gopnik revealed that babies are sensitive to emotion and 14-month-olds show empathy. They will cross a room to give you a pen if you drop one. Highly sensitive people seem to have simply retained this intense sense of connection to others.

But knowing that we feel and experience empathy more deeply doesn't mean we have to act on it. We may be more sensitive and feel more than others, but we still have a choice as to what we do with those feelings.

What I learned

I feel lucky to be such an empathic person. It makes me feel good knowing that I have genuine concern and compassion for people. I enjoy listening and being there for others. And I know they appreciate it too. But I've learned that it can be all too easy to slip into enabling and dependent behaviours that are self-sacrificing and ultimately damaging. Here are a few things I have learned about managing empathy as an HSP.

1 **Take care of yourself first.** Highly sensitive people are empathic, caring and emotional, but you need to have empathy and compassion for yourself as much as anyone else. This sounds simple, but for many highly sensitive people, it can feel strange and selfish. We seem to be built for giving, so much so that we can forget about our own needs. It's easy to get sucked into other people's feelings and their lives and problems and find yourself attached to them, especially when they tell you how much better they feel when you're there. You feel good because you're

helping them. They feel better because you're absorbing all their negative feelings like a vacuum cleaner. They end up feeling clean and tidy and you feel like an overstuffed vacuum bag.

The key is to remember that the best person to protect your sensitive self is you. Recognize that you can serve others better when you're feeling good about yourself. If you don't feel good about yourself, put your time and energy into sorting yourself out before you take on anyone else's issues. When people come to you with their problems, be honest with them and yourself about your own limits. Don't give till it hurts. You are wired for compassion, but you need compassion too.

2   **Know that you're not responsible for anyone else.** Just because you feel someone else's feelings doesn't mean you have to do anything about it. This can feel incredibly counter-intuitive. When I sense that someone needs help or is suffering in some emotional way, even if they don't say so, I always feel as if I'm standing over someone who's lying in the street in front on an oncoming vehicle. I can't just walk away. Can I? The answer is yes. You might feel that you have to help, but you don't. You're not responsible for anyone else. You can help if you want to, but help in a way that won't hurt you. Throw them a life preserver, make them a cup of tea, offer comforting words, call an ambulance, give them a blanket, but don't go running into oncoming traffic. Ultimately, people have to help themselves. And you have to look after your sensitive self. Empathy is good. Throwing yourself in front of a bus is not.

3   **Avoid energy vampires.** Sadly, there are some people who will want to use your sensitivity and empathy for their own good. In *Emotional Vampires*, Albert Bernstein provides some excellent suggestions for learning how to detect and deal with these energy vampires. Vampire is another word for vacuum cleaner or narcissist. Whatever you call them, they will suck you dry. It can be hard to recognize them because they are usually masters of deception and manipulation. One of Bernstein's suggestions is paying attention to people's actions, not their words. These kinds of people will say anything to get you to do what they want, so don't believe everything they say. If you have low self-esteem, they will tell you things you are desperate to hear to win your loyalty. They will tell you you're smart and pretty and a

wonderful person, just so that you feel good around them. If you put your energy into building your self-confidence instead, you won't need anyone to tell you how great you are because you'll already know.

4 **Pause and reflect.** The key to dealing with other people is to check in with your own feelings. Use your sensitivity to pause and reflect before acting. According to Elaine Aron in *The Highly Sensitive Person*, this 'pause-to-check' system is a key HSP trait, which makes us stop and wait until we understand a new circumstance. We naturally tend to stop and think before acting, so don't feel pressured into doing something faster than you want to. Ask yourself how you're feeling. If someone or something is making you feel sad, uncomfortable, anxious or unhappy, it's your sensitivity telling you there's a problem. Someone might be saying they need you, they love you, they think you're wonderful, there's nothing wrong, but trust your own instincts. Remember, highly sensitive people have unique brains that can pick up on subtleties. If it doesn't feel right, say no and walk away. I know it's not easy. But it will be easier to bear than the soul-destroying siege of sacrificing yourself for someone else.

5 **Let go of other people's feelings.** I read a book called *Empowered by Empathy* by Rose Rosetree and found some really useful suggestions for distinguishing my emotions from other people's. If you're experiencing strong emotions and you're not sure where they are coming from, don't try to ignore them or succumb to their power over you. Feelings are an important part of your intelligence and your special gifts. Sit down somewhere quiet and close your eyes. Take a few deep breaths until you feel calm. Then ask yourself, 'What am I feeling right now?' Sit still and wait for an answer. Don't force it. It will come to you. Then ask yourself: 'Who am I empathically connected to right now?' Again, wait for an answer. It could come as a thought, a name, an image. This process taps into your subconscious mind, where all the information you absorb resides. Whenever I've done this, it happens really fast. I tend to see ideas as images, so I will get a photo or movie of someone behaving angrily, for example, and when I ask the second question, I get a head shot, a school portrait of the person who owns those feelings. The next step is to say to yourself: 'This does not belong to me. Please leave immediately.'

Finally, take a deep breath. Think about who you are, your mind, your body, your own emotions. Take another deep breath and open your eyes. This may sound very voodoo, but it's really about connecting to your own intuition, your own mind, and letting go of the stuff that is hurtful to you. Words and intentions have enormous power. High sensitivity is also powerful. Use that to help yourself heal.

6   **Channel your compassion into work.** It's hard to go against your own nature, so my advice is, don't. You can't change who you really are. And I think it's important to be who you really are. Most HSPs spend our lives trying to be something else, trying to fit in with what's acceptable. I say, don't. The best thing you can do is be yourself. And instead of focusing your energy on people who should be helping themselves, direct your natural empathy and compassion into a worthy cause where it will really do some good without hurting you. This might be channelling your empathy into helping professions like counselling, psychology, teaching or parenting your children. Or you might help animals, the environment or other charitable causes in your spare time. When you use your natural abilities to make the world a better place, you will feel the joy, rather than the pain, of giving. And thrive.

7
Relationships

'When someone shows you who they are, believe them the first time.'

Maya Angelou

I'm 26 and living in Vancouver. I have a boyfriend who doesn't really like his job and wants to find another one, but he isn't sure what he wants to do or what he'll be good at. I care about him and want him to be happy so I try to help him. I love him so much I feel as though it is me who is struggling to find the right career, who's frustrated by the limitations of my current position, who is confused about where I should go next.

So I search the want-ads and websites, read career books, edit his resumé and coach him on his interview skills. And when he finally gets a new job, I am so happy, I fall to the floor in tears of joy and relief. I feel like *I* have landed that job. I am so excited, I seem to be expressing all the feelings he has inside but can't or won't express, as if his feelings are living outside of him and inside of me. I have become the embodiment and expression of his emotions and his needs.

In the meantime, I happily put my own career aspirations aside so that I can focus on helping him. For some reason I don't understand, I can feel his worry and his struggles more than my own. For some reason, they seem more important than mine. I feel compelled to help him because not helping would make me feel I was hurting him and I couldn't live with that.

So when we break up a year later, I feel not only that I've lost someone special, but that I've lost a part of myself.

Making sense of sensitivity

Relationships can be both wonderful and challenging for highly sensitive people. When they're healthy, this is where highly sensitive people really show their strengths. We love the intimacy of one-to-one connections. With good listening and communication skills, matched to genuine care and concern for others' well-being, personal relationships give us a chance to blossom.

But highly sensitive people tend to reflect more and worry about how things are going more than other people, says Elaine Aron in *The Highly Sensitive Person in Love*. We also tend to feel more threatened or anxious when things go wrong or when we notice flaws in our partner or their behaviour. This is a natural consequence of the HSP traits of noticing subtleties, absorbing information and processing deeply. We don't choose to think or act this way. It's just the way we are. But it can make us feel nervous, worried or afraid when we are in a relationship. And that anxiety and attention to detail can be disruptive to the peace and comfort we're seeking.

Relationships with other highly sensitive people can seem like the ideal solution. But not all highly sensitive people get into relationships with other highly sensitive people. In fact, I think it's quite rare. This is partly because highly sensitive people can be hard to find. We're not often out and about, socializing and meeting people. You're more likely to find an HSP at the library or an art class or writers' group. Even if two HSPs do get together, there's no guaranteed success. Two sensitive people can offer each other great understanding and depth, but it can also be suffocating. There's also the problem of dealing with two HSPs' own issues with low self-esteem, depression, anxiety and feeling overwhelmed.

What happens more often, I think, is that highly sensitive people find themselves in relationships with non-HSPs, and unfortunately, with people who are more interested in getting their own needs met than caring about their partner. Highly sensitive people are compassionate, gentle, and emotional human beings who feel other people's feelings. Consequently, this can make us vulnerable to people who want to take advantage of our sensitivity and susceptible to being taken for granted, especially when we put their needs before our own.

Longing for intimacy

Everyone needs to feel loved. Humans are hardwired to seek and cherish a deep sense of love and connection. We need other people in our lives to feel a sense of belonging and understanding, as well as the intimacy of a relationship with one special person. Highly sensitive people need other people too. We just don't need as many. And we need the relationships we do have to be deep, loving, authentic and close. Superficial relationships just don't work for us.

In my own romantic relationships and friendships, people have valued this quality in me. They like to feel close too and to know that my feelings for them are genuine. They appreciate that our relationship is based on real emotions. They know that, for me, a relationship is about a continual process of learning, understanding and connecting to the other person.

For many people, however, this kind of intimacy is frightening. This is because intimacy and connection require us to be open, and this makes us vulnerable. Most people want to feel loved and to feel close to their partner, but for some, the fear of exposure and the potential for rejection are too great. The kind of deep and meaningful relationship that HSPs crave can be just too much for some people. Because we're aware of people's feelings and subtle changes in their mood, highly sensitive people also want to help. But some people don't want to reveal their painful feelings or discuss their difficult experiences. So this disparity can lead to conflict.

When there is conflict, highly sensitive people need a lot of quiet time on their own to recover. Sometimes this can make a partner feel left out. It can be very difficult for non-HSPs to understand why we need so much downtime. They might think we're angry with them or giving them the cold shoulder. And when we've recharged and made up, we might prefer a walk in the park or a quiet dinner to a big night out to celebrate.

Feeling connected to kids

The HSP need for authentic, loving connections with people is part of the reason why I think highly sensitive people often have good relationships with children. Kids have an uncanny ability to see through people. They know when you're being fake, when you're pretending to be happy even when you're not, or when you say you like children when you really don't. They know the truth. Highly sensitive people value genuine relationships and children pick up on this. I think kids are also attracted to an HSP's caring nature, compassion and empathy. They seem to be able to see it before anyone else does. I've met children who understood who I was and what I was all about ten minutes after meeting me, while most adults never do. Children have a natural intuitive sense about people, just as highly sensitive people do.

Like children, highly sensitive people are open to the world, seeing things as they really are without the limitations and restrictions of bias, prejudice or bitterness. We accept people as they are, and can see behind the masks that people wear. We are creative and imaginative and we can see the possibilities in everything.

I used to wonder when I was going to 'grow up' and become an adult like everyone else. I worried about it because I wanted to fit in, even if that meant losing my sense of playfulness. But eventually I realized that I was never going to become that kind of adult. I also realized that I was actually quite mature, logical and intelligent. The difference was that, unlike many non-HSPs, I was always going to retain my openness, empathy and creativity.

At the same time, highly sensitive people often feel enormous concern for children. Perhaps this is because we feel so connected to them and because our natural empathic abilities mean we cannot stand to see children suffer. I can't bear the glass-shattering screams of babies or the endless wails of small children because the sound is overwhelming. But the worst part is that I can feel their feelings. I can feel how unhappy, tired, frustrated or lonely they are. And it hurts.

Avoiding confrontation

Highly sensitive people are not only *aware* of emotions, we *feel* them intensely. Whether they are our own or someone else's, feelings have the power to lift us up or drag us down. When conflicts, misunderstandings and problems arise in relationships and things become stressful or heated, we can quickly become overwhelmed. All we want is for everyone to kiss and make up and feel happy again.

Consequently, highly sensitive people tend to avoid conflicts at all costs. We try to talk things out, but often give in to the other person to avoid an argument. We walk away from disagreements rather than fight. We bend under a dominant person's will because the negative feelings are too much to bear.

What this means, unfortunately, is that highly sensitive people often have a hard time standing up for themselves and for their own needs. It also means that malicious people will take advantage of our need for peace and harmony in order to assert their authority and need for control.

Mistreated by narcissists

Because highly sensitive people are compassionate and eager to help, we are often targets for narcissists. These are people who have an exaggerated sense of their own importance, who are obsessed with power, and believe they are entitled to special privileges. They constantly seek admiration and attention and they exploit others for their own ends, with complete lack of empathy for the feelings or needs of others. Narcissists take advantage of us, drain our energy and take our kindness without giving anything in return. They are also experts at manipulation and control, deception, and passive-aggressive behaviour, so that most HSPs don't even realize they've been taken in by a narcissist until it's too late. Highly sensitive people don't consciously choose this kind of relationship, but we are very vulnerable to it.

At first, narcissists can seem nice, funny, charming, generous, and appreciative of your sensitive, caring, giving nature. But before you know it, you are living with someone who only wants you to cater to their every need. Narcissists will use praise or flattery to coerce sensitive people. This makes us feel good about ourselves. We feel needed and so we give more.

But as this pattern continues, we end up giving until we've got nothing left. The narcissist creates a relationship with the sensitive person that essentially allows them to feed off the kindness of the HSP, to satisfy their insatiable appetite for praise,

dmiration, power, money and material things until
ensitive partner is left emotionally drained, exhausted
ess. This feeling of helplessness also helps to explain
why it is so hard for HSPs to leave these kinds of relationships.
Unfortunately, HSPs often believe that if we just give a little more,
try a little harder, it will be enough. But it's never enough. The
narcissist always wants more.

Narcissists disrespect our boundaries, blame us, criticize us
and make us feel so bad about ourselves that we don't have the
energy to leave the relationship. So we stay and try harder as our
self-esteem continues to sink further.

Sabotaged by our subconscious

It's not only relationships with narcissists that can cause our self-
confidence to plummet. As we discussed in Chapter 5 on low
self-esteem, many highly sensitive people learn to feel insecure
because we are different and often unaccepted for who we are.
Without accepting ourselves as strong, capable and worthy
individuals, we can easily experience chronic low self-esteem and
bring our feelings of self-doubt into our relationships with others,
where it causes further problems.

Just as an HSP can be lured into relationships with narcissists, they can also be drawn to people who share their feelings
of self-doubt. No matter who we are, our subconscious minds
draw us to people who reflect our own beliefs about ourselves.
So the powerful attraction you feel towards someone may
really be more of a sense of familiarity. We find that comforting
because we are all attracted to what's familiar to us, whether
that's good or bad. That's why many children of alcoholics grow
up to marry alcoholics. It's not that they enjoy the alcoholic
lifestyle. It's just what they're used to. Subconsciously, it feels
like home. And we all do it. According to Dr Harville Hendrix,
author of *Getting the Love You Want*, if you have needs that have
been neglected, you are going to continue to seek out people
who make you feel the same way as you did when you were
growing up, so that you can try to relive the experience and
finally get what you need.

While this idea seems rather hopeless, it also means that you can and should stop blaming yourself for 'choosing' to be with someone who is an alcoholic or a narcissist or a pathological liar. It wasn't a conscious choice. Your brain is hardwired to try to re-enact your childhood relationship dynamics so that you can attempt to resolve the issues from your past. If you felt ignored as a child, for example, you will continually seek out people who ignore you so that you can change them with your undying love and finally receive the attention you crave. Unfortunately, these are the people who are usually the least able to give you what you need.

For highly sensitive people, this subconscious pull can often mean we're drawn towards people who also have low self-esteem, who don't understand themselves or who don't like who they are. People with insecurities are often attracted to HSPs because we're willing to listen and because we show genuine empathy and care. For many people who are struggling, HSPs can feel like a warm blanket or a soft place to fall. And we HSPs often want to be there to catch them. Unfortunately, playing the role of someone else's safety net doesn't work well for long. Over time, we become weaker and more damaged.

Psychologist Deirdre Lovecky (1993) says that gifted people often repress their own needs so that they can develop connections to others. Highly sensitive people are often gifted. We're creative and empathic, but we're also gifted in ways others don't always see or appreciate. We only know that we're different and we don't fit in. Consequently, says Lovecky, we feel we must choose between loneliness and denying our own needs, our own self.

What I learned

I've learned a lot about relationships through my own experiences, making mistakes, getting rejected and trying to please others – in other words, the hard way. I've also learned through my curiosity and need to understand, which has led me to read and research until things make sense. For me, understanding why things happen the way they do is the key to coping emotionally. If I can understand it, I can deal with it. It doesn't mean everything will work out the way I want it to, but it means that I can accept things for what they really are, not what I fear.

I hope, other sensitive people will learn from my experiences and mistakes, as well as their own, and find the healthy, happy relationships they deserve.

1   **Remember that you don't need anyone's approval.** You don't need to depend on other people to tell you you're a good person in order to feel good about yourself. You don't need others to thank you for helping them and you don't need to help other people so that you can feel needed. Relying on someone else to make you believe you're worthwhile will only make you dependent on them, and then you will become a victim once again.

Instead of looking to others to give you the validation, approval, acceptance and love you need, give it to yourself. You've got it all inside you. Show up on the doorstep of relationships with everything you need in your own back pocket. Know that you are a good and kind person, that you are capable of enormous compassion and love and know that you deserve love, compassion and respect in return. If the other person doesn't reflect that in the way they treat you, it's time to leave. You don't need anyone's approval but your own.

2   **Avoid narcissists.** You need to realize that highly sensitive people are vulnerable to narcissists in ways that others are not. But that does not make you powerless. You are a delicate creature so you must protect yourself. Instead of seeing your sensitivity as a fault or a weakness, use your unique qualities to see others for what they really are and trust your own amazing sense of intuition and awareness to identify their true feelings, as well as your own. Beware of people who seem a little too preoccupied with their appearance, their status and what people think of them. A series of studies by Konrath et al. (2014) revealed that one simple question will identify a narcissist – ask them if they're a narcissist. A narcissistic person will say yes because they're not ashamed of their narcissistic personality. They're proud of it.

3   **Never try to 'fix' anyone.** Don't think you can change someone. You can't. People can only fix themselves. People can change, but only if they want to. If you think you are in a relationship with a narcissist or someone who is not treating you well, don't try to fix them. Don't try to win them over with your love. It won't work.

Just walk away. Find someone who will treat you with respect. You deserve it. If the narcissist is your mother or some other person you can't or don't want to eliminate from your life completely, accept them for who they are and put up some clear boundaries between you. They will not change. They don't want to change. Narcissists don't think there's anything wrong with them.

The truth is that a narcissist is never going to give you what you need. Avoiding and denying that fact is easier, but it's only going to fuel their fire and make you feel like a doormat. The alternative, acceptance, is harder, but it works. Accept that they will never change. Accept that you will never get love from them. And accept that you deserve love, and can get it, from someone else. Love yourself by demonstrating that you will only accept kind, loving, respectful relationships. And then others will love you too.

It's not easy to walk away and choose to be alone. I have stayed in relationships long after their expiration date because I wanted them to work. But this isn't just about fear. In their book *Attached: The New Science of Adult Attachment and How It Can Help You Find and Keep Love*, authors Amir Levine and Rachel Heller explain that our brains are hard-wired to seek the support of our partner during times of stress. We were never meant to endure all of life's trials alone. But this dependence means that our partner's feelings, moods and behaviour affect us. And when our attempts at closeness fail, we become increasingly needy and anxious and more likely to stay in unhealthy relationships. But we can't live with someone who is narcissistic, for example, and expect ourselves to simply ignore their antics and satisfy our own needs. A healthy relationship hinges on *both* partners' ability to give and receive support. If you are doing all the giving, it's time to move on and find someone who will be there for you when you need them.

'All you can hope for', says psychologist Harville Hendrix in his book *Keeping the Love You Find*, 'is to find someone who is aware of his or her problems and willing to do, with you, the hard work necessary to heal.'

4 **Develop healthy boundaries.** Boundaries are healthy limits we set between ourselves and other people. They define what we are comfortable with and what we are not. And because we absorb so much of what's happening around us, including the feelings

and energies of other people, boundaries are essential for highly sensitive people.

Relationships test our boundaries, so it's important to know where to draw the line. The key is to listen to your own feelings. No matter what anyone else tells you, if it feels bad, it's bad for you. That's it. The challenge comes not only in establishing boundaries, but maintaining them. It's one thing to draw the line. But what happens when someone crosses it? When this happens, many of us, HSPs and non-HSPs alike, can feel taken advantage of and victimized. Sometimes we are afraid to enforce our boundaries and say no for fear of losing that person's love. But real love does not make you afraid. Real love accepts you and respects your needs.

The key to maintaining boundaries is to have consequences for crossing them. People will often test you to see whether your boundaries are weak or strong, and whether you really mean what you say. You just have to be clear. If your partner always wants you to go out when you don't want to, for example, and you find it upsetting, you need to talk about it and be clear about your needs. Tell them how you feel and then explain that if they bully you again, you will not go out with them anymore. You may decide to go out occasionally, but say that you'll arrange for your own ride home so you can leave when you want to. Decide what will work for you and make it clear and then stick to it. In a good relationship, both partners will respect each other's boundaries. If your partner continually crosses the line, you may be involved with someone who doesn't respect you, in which case it may not be the right relationship for you. By setting and maintaining clear boundaries, it will be a lot easier to avoid the wrong people and find the right ones.

I learned a lot about boundaries by reading the book *Boundaries: When to Say Yes, When to Say No to Take Control of Your Life* by Henry Cloud and John Townsend. The light really came on, however, when I found myself at the tail end of another relationship and realized that I really was okay on my own. I realized that, despite my fears, being alone was better than being in a bad relationship and that I was, in fact, happier on my own, doing what I liked to do and spending time with people who accepted me for who I am.

5 **Tell your partner what you need.** Don't expect anyone to read your mind. Make sure people understand your needs by

explaining them clearly. Begging someone to be nicer to you will not work. Be clear and specific. Tell them that you need time alone after a day out, you don't enjoy noisy events and you're crying because the sound of the neighbour's hedge trimmer is destroying your brain. Whatever it is you need, it's important that you communicate that to your partner. Not expressing your needs and then getting upset about it is more stressful for everyone and leads to miscommunication and frustration. Ultimately, it's up to you to make sure you get your needs met, so knowing what works for you and what doesn't can give you that authority. Expressing your needs clearly means that people who care about you will be able to give you what you need. And sometimes what HSPs need most of all is simply understanding.

When you take responsibility for your life, by expressing what you need and how you feel, an amazing thing happens. You build your self-esteem because you are saying that your needs are important. At the same time, if your partner can give you what you need, such as taking you to the park when the neighbours are having a party or letting you soak in the tub while they look after the kids, they'll also be helping themselves to grow. They'll get the love, respect and trust from you that they need. What one partner needs most is often in the precise area where the other partner needs to grow, says Hendrix. But, to work, it takes both of you expressing your needs and helping each other.

6   **Face your feelings.** Since highly sensitive people are prone to low self-esteem, we tend to blame ourselves when relationships go wrong. We believe we could've done something differently to fix it. But other people also have their own issues. They have their own hang-ups and insecurities and problems. They need to sort out their own emotions and you need to deal with yours. This is why I read articles and books, write in a journal, cry, talk, read some more, make notes, spend hours staring out of the window thinking, cry some more and write some more until my feelings and my motives make sense. And then I can let the negative emotions go. Perhaps more importantly, when I've faced my feelings and accepted them, they let go of me.

7   **Don't take on other people's 'stuff'.** Most of the issues that other people have have nothing to do with you. Anything anyone says about you is about them, not you. It's simply an

expression of who they are, what they're feeling, what they want. Sometimes their criticisms or judgments of you may be right. Sometimes they aren't. But it's up to you to decide what you want to take on and what to leave with them. Words can hurt. But knowing that hurtful words belong to someone else can stop them from sinking in too deep. Take the criticism that will help you grow and learn, and leave the rest.

8 **Respond to the present, not to the past.** Just as other people's behaviour is about them, your behaviour is about you. For example, if someone says something that upsets you, you might be angry or upset with that person. But your emotional reaction is based on your own needs, your own fears, and your own unresolved issues. It may seem as though the other person is causing us to feel annoyed or hurt, but they are probably just triggering a memory or a feeling from your past and that's why it hurts. If your brother always called you names, for example, and it hurt your feelings, you're probably going to get upset whenever someone teases you, even if they don't mean any harm. If your feelings about this remain unresolved, you're going to become increasingly unsettled by it.

Highly sensitive people will always be more emotional and feel things more intensely than others, but we don't have to be more hurt by people. Your response to emotional triggers is your response to the past. Instead of reacting to pain from the past, we can choose to respond to the present. Highly sensitive people may be wired for wonder, but that doesn't mean we have to stay trapped in a childlike state of helplessness. We need to protect ourselves by responding like an adult.

You can do that by recognizing the words, attitudes or expressions that trigger your emotional response. You can learn to recognize your personal triggers by becoming aware of your feelings and your physiological reactions, such as shaky hands, sweaty palms or a racing heart. Noticing your own body's response can tell you when something painful from your past has been triggered. When something triggers your fear, you may experience the same feelings you had as a child when you were hurt, angry or afraid, such as feeling anxious, helpless, unworthy or powerless. These feelings make it very difficult to respond to the present moment in an effective way because it means you're dependent on someone else to make you feel better. The key to changing your reactions and preventing conflict involves awareness of your reactions and making the choice to respond to what's actually happening now in a calm, considered way. You may need to take a break and just breathe deeply until you feel calmer and can think more clearly about what *you* want to do next.

Someone who is not consistently there for you will trigger your anxieties and fears more often. If you feel anxious or insecure in a relationship, it's a sign that the other person is not safe. A safe person will respond to your emotional needs with calm reassurance, say psychologists Henry Cloud and John Townsend in *Safe People*.

As a highly sensitive adult, you can take care of your childhood pain by responding in an adult way, by expressing your needs (without being demanding), listening to (not blaming or ignoring) the other person, and coming up with a resolution that may involve more communication or ending the relationship. But responding to a current situation as if it were the past will make you feel like an anxious, insecure, needy child. Responding to the present will make you feel safe, secure, confident and calm because *you* are looking after *yourself*. When you do, you can improve your relationships and heal.

9 **Find a partner who suits you.** In her book, *The Highly Sensitive Person in Love*, Elaine Aron suggests that highly sensitive people might be better off with a non-HSP partner because two HSPs might become bored, stay at home too much and use each other as a sanctuary. On the other hand, she says, two HSPs are more likely to understand each other, recognize each other's traits and habits and develop a more supportive and peaceful partnership. They will also be likely to enjoy similar interests and want to live life at the same thoughtful pace. Whether you choose a fellow HSP or a non-HSP, however, depends on what works best for you. What matters is how you feel when you're with that person and whether they accept, value, respect and love you for who you are, a sensitive person who is wired for wonder.

8
Socializing

'Innovators and creators are persons who can to a higher degree than average accept the condition of aloneness. They are more willing to follow their own vision, even when it takes them far from the mainland of the human community.'

Nathaniel Branden

I have been living in the UK for about a year when I decide to join a walking group. I am living in West Oxfordshire, not far from the Cotswolds. It's a beautiful area that I want to explore more and so I think a walking group will be a good way to meet new people.

It's a sunny Sunday in June and I drive out to a car park by a cricket field in Minster Lovell, a village on the river Windrush where I am supposed to meet up with about 20 strangers and go for a walk. There are already a few people there when I arrive and I nervously say hello. The group has a website and I scan the faces, trying to match them up with the names and photos I've seen online, but none of them look familiar.

After a few minutes, one woman introduces herself to me and begins to talk about the walk. I don't recognize her, but I remember her name. As she talks, I realize she must've posted a picture of herself on the website from about 20 years ago. When I speak to her, she tells me that she was very good-looking when she was young, so she wanted to post a photo of herself from her youth. That makes it rather difficult for new members to recognize her now, though, doesn't it? I'm new to this walking group thing, however, and I begin to think that maybe appearances matter more than I thought.

We set off on the walk and I get talking with some other women in the group. Everyone seems to pair up as we follow a narrow path along a field edge and then down into some woods. I listen as a woman tells me about her funeral director business and then someone else tells me about her cycling holiday in Spain. Another woman talks to me about her running injuries. It's fun and exciting meeting new people and hearing about their lives and all their experiences. But I begin to feel that I'm missing the walk. My attention to whoever is speaking to me keeps drawing me away from the views of the hills and the trees and the bright summer sunlight that has settled on the river as we cross the bridge. And after a while, I begin to feel my shoulders rising up to my ears and my hands clenching into tight little balls as the steady stream of words and small talk pushes away the birdsong and fills my mind like clutter.

As we climb out of a valley to a hilltop to rest, another woman begins talking to me and I wonder how much longer the walk will be. She tells me how much she loves music and going to concerts and relays a list of all the bands she's been to see. She also tells me she's married.

'Where's your husband?' I ask, looking around at the unlikely candidates.

'Oh, he's not here,' she says. 'He doesn't like groups. So I just come on my own.'

I nod and smile and keep listening as she talks some more, but she has said something that has made me understand something about myself and what I'm doing with my life. It has connected with me so deeply, it feels like a door opening. In that moment, I realize I'm more like this woman's husband than her. I don't like groups either. And then I wonder what the hell I'm doing there, wandering around the countryside with a big group when every moment is making me feel more stressed. They all seem like nice, friendly people. But they all want to talk and they all want to belong to a group. I only joined this group so that I could meet people, a person in fact, and then leave once I'd found a kindred spirit, someone I could really connect with. It hadn't occurred to me that everyone else intended to join the group and stay there forever. But they do it because they like groups. For me, it was more like a necessary evil.

Standing on that hill, staring out at the clouds that hover in the bright blue sky like water lilies in a still pond, I listen to everyone talking and laughing as we wait for the stragglers to make it to the top, and I realize that, while I need people and a sense of belonging as well, I just don't need as many or as much. What I'm longing for isn't company, but closeness, connection and the intimacy of feeling understood.

After five miles, the walk is over and we end up back at the parking lot, where everyone decides to go for lunch at a nearby pub. I thank them and tell them I'm sorry but I have to get home. I've been listening to people talk for nearly three hours and I have to get away. The sun is still out and I can't bear the thought of sitting inside at a table full of people.

I say goodbye, get in my car and drive home and when I get inside, I take off my boots and cling to the kitchen counter as the stress of socializing pours out of me in long wet tears. It isn't what I wanted. But I feel saturated with other people's energy. I dry my face, put my boots back on and go out for another walk, this time on my own, until at last I feel that I can breathe.

Making sense of sensitivity

Most highly sensitive people are introverts, so we enjoy spending time at home, doing quiet, thinking, introspective things. It's not that we're afraid to go out or meet new people, it's that we find socializing very draining. When I think of how stressful social-izing can be, I often think of the famous saying by Jean-Paul Sartre that my highly sensitive dad used to quote: 'Hell is other people'.

Everyday stress also means that we need a lot of time to recharge, and we do that by spending time alone or with just one other person. Consequently, we tend to avoid social activities. Sometimes, this can make life challenging. Highly sensitive people like to engage with others and have fun, but we can only cope with society in small doses, for limited amounts of time, before we begin to feel overwhelmed and frazzled.

For me, spending time with a group of people, no matter how nice or friendly or fun they are, makes me begin to feel that I'm being grabbed and poked and prodded, as if their words are physical things jabbing my senses and scratching at my skin. After a while, I just can't take any more.

When I talk to just one person, however, I enjoy the conversation. I love stimulating discussions. I don't feel overwhelmed. It's not an assault on my senses. HSPs usually prefer these kinds of intimate connections with others because it's less overwhelming and because it's an opportunity to discuss things in depth. We're not interested in superficial things or small talk. We don't care about shoes or football results or who's said what. We don't like gossip. We want to know what's really going on, what people really think and feel. We have an insatiable curiosity, a genuine passion for understanding people and a need to discover hidden meanings. We want to see the truth behind the facade. Skimming the surface only leads to frustration.

Sporting events are particularly toxic to me. I quickly become overwhelmed by the energy and emotions and the noise of the crowds of team sports. Even a television commercial for a sporting event will make me run out of the room. I can't take the announcer's shouting, the fans roaring, the clapping and cheering. I can't bear it because the noise and energy of it makes me feel that someone is clawing at my nerves. It must have been a highly sensitive person who invented the mute button.

I prefer solo activities like running, walking, swimming and cycling. As a child, I hated gym class, although I was fairly athletic. I despised the competitiveness of the games. Once we were told we were going outside to play baseball as a treat. After all the other kids ran out of the classroom in a fit of excited shrieks, I asked if I could stay behind and read instead. Even the teacher thought that was weird.

A study by Mehl and Vazire (2010) showed that perhaps highly sensitive people understand happiness better than most. In their research, the authors found that people are happier when they have less small talk and more deep and meaningful conversations. Whether you're highly sensitive or not, the researchers discovered, it's not just socializing that matters, it's how *connected* you feel to other people. In our pursuit of in-depth, one-to-one conversations, highly sensitive people are not trying to avoid people; we're trying to feel more connected to them because it makes us happy.

Nevertheless, many people find HSPs difficult to understand. We tend not to share our thoughts and feelings openly with just anyone. We can't do too many things in one day. We don't like to be rushing around, participating, socializing, flitting from one activity to the next. It's just too exhausting for our sensitive selves. So we have to say no and decline invitations sometimes. But we love being alone. We find it peaceful, and it gives us a chance to think, reflect and process everything we've absorbed. Highly sensitive people need that.

Some non-HSP friends have told me they always need to be busy because they don't like to be alone. While I sometimes envy their active social lives and their endless invitations, they have surprised me by saying how much they envy my ability to spend time alone, to enjoy my own company, to have the courage to just be by myself. One study (Wilson 2014) actually found that most people would rather give themselves an electric shock than be left alone with their thoughts.

Unfortunately, highly sensitive people can often be misunderstood and judged as being aloof, snobbish, cold, fearful or arrogant. People often judge you harshly for declining invitations or leaving the party early. I once invited an Avon lady to my house, and as I sat there listening to her and looking at all her cosmetics, she told me that she was nervous. When I asked her why, she said my quietness was intimidating. Of course, I wasn't trying to intimidate her, but the reticence of HSPs can, to some people, seem as if we're silently judging them when, in fact, we're deeply listening. I felt so bad that I ended up buying far too much expensive hand cream.

Consequently, for many highly sensitive people, finding those opportunities for in-depth, close and stimulating one-to-one conversations can be challenging. We're often trapped in a world of longing for connection, but shattered by interaction. We love the peace and quiet that solitude provides and the necessary space it gives us to be thoughtful and creative. At the same time, we can feel like outsiders, looking in on a social world we're not part of, pressing our noses against the glass, unseen, unheard and often unaccepted by those inside. For sensitive women in particular, a lack of solitude can increase the risk of developing depression and other disorders, suggests psychologist Kathleen Noble, perhaps as an unconscious way of trying to create the personal space they need.

Not all highly sensitive people are introverts, however. According to Elaine Aron (1996), 30 per cent of highly sensitive people are extraverts, although each of our personalities appears somewhere on the spectrum of extraversion and introversion to varying degrees, rather than at one extreme or the other. Introversion and extraversion are terms first developed by Carl Jung and explain where people get their energy. People who are more introverted are rejuvenated by spending time alone, while extraverts are energized by spending time with people. They like to be involved in lots of events and social activities and feel excited when they can energize others. Typically, introverts prefer to think about ideas, while extraverts understand their world by talking things out.

Each of these personality types presents its own challenges as well. While highly sensitive introverts often run the risk of becoming too withdrawn and isolated, sensitive extraverts can easily become overwhelmed by too many social activities. HSP extraverts enjoy group activities like all extraverts, but they also need time alone to recover from the stimulation of being around other people.

What I learned

Highly sensitive people are often mistakenly thought of as too shy, insecure or timid to get out there and join in. The truth is that, for introverts, we just don't want to. We're happy doing our own thing. But we also want a connection with others and to have opportunities to talk about meaningful things and ideas. Here's what I've learned about finding some happy middle ground.

1 **Find an HSP or introverted friend.** Since introverts tend to be good listeners and enjoy one-to-one conversations, highly sensitive people can often find the compassion and understanding they're looking for in another highly sensitive person or introvert. This applies to HSP extraverts as well, who may need a quiet friend to discuss their thoughts and feelings with. It's important to have someone who understands you and your sensitive trait to talk to so that you can be open and be yourself, without feeling that you have to hide your personality or explain your actions.

Give yourself opportunities to express your true feelings and the unique way you see the world. Highly sensitive people can be hard to find, but book clubs, writers' groups, art classes and personal development seminars are good places to start.

2 **Find a cause.** Despite our need for solitude and quiet time, highly sensitive people are usually bursting with insights, ideas and a drive to make the world a better place. Whether you're an introvert or an extravert, use your high sensitivity to express your passion for causes you believe in and make things happen. This is a great way to meet like-minded people because you'll share an interest as well as a commitment to helping others. Highly sensitive people are often outraged by the suffering of other people and animals, so use that energy for the greater good and everyone will feel better, including you.

3 **Be yourself.** Highly sensitive people aren't like other people. Lots of parties, outings, gatherings and events just aren't our idea of a good time. It's okay to say no. Don't fall into the trap of saying yes to every invitation or trying to fit in. Most of the world's population are non-HSP extraverts, so it can be tempting to bury your sensitive side to gain a sense of belonging. But as a highly sensitive person, you have different needs.

Tell your friends and family you just need some regular downtime. And then use this time to think and reflect, meditate, garden, go for a walk, or do something creative and be sure to get enough sleep. You need to be aware of what drains you and what energizes you and then give yourself permission to avoid or do those things. It's easy to fall into the habit of doing things because you always have or because your friends like doing them or because your mother thinks it will be good for you. But if you don't take care of your sensitivity, you won't have anything to give to others.

When you feel rejuvenated again, try looking for activities that suit you. I need low levels of sensory stimulation but high amounts of mental stimulation. So that means I avoid sporting events, music festivals and anything involving audience participation. But I like to meet a friend for coffee to talk or visit a historic site or take an interesting class where I can learn. I find group discussions tend to float on top of the issues I'm eager to dive down deep into, so I try to find activities that involve one-to-one conversations. I also like to read and watch documentaries and think about and discuss them.

4 **Find a balance.** Socializing as a highly sensitive person often means that we swing from being out too much or in too much. We feel pulled by social convention to participate in activities, only to feel exhausted and resentful afterwards. Or we avoid going out to protect ourselves from the inevitable feeling of being overwhelmed and end up feeling isolated and lonely.

One study (House et al. 1988) showed that a lack of social connection is worse for your health than obesity, smoking and high blood pressure. It also makes you more vulnerable to anxiety and depression. Another study (Lee et al. 2001) revealed that people who feel more connected to others have lower rates of anxiety and higher self-esteem.

Finding the balance between the two extremes of isolation and integration is the way to cope. The key is to figure out how much social interaction and quiet time you need. If you're an extraverted HSP, you may need to socialize more often. As an introverted HSP, you might have to learn to say no to social pressure. Don't be afraid to give yourself whatever you need. It's not how many friends you have that counts. It's the quality of the connection that matters.

9
Work

'The best prize that life has to offer is to work hard at work worth doing.'

Theodore Roosevelt

I'm 28 when I start working for a magazine publishing company as an editor. The office is set up in a converted warehouse on the outskirts of Toronto. It has high ceilings that seem to drip with thick, grey stucco and florescent lights that swing like lifeboats over my head.

It's winter, and when I come to work, I leave my coat and gloves on. The surface of my desk is like a frozen pond. I work in a cubicle, a cosy little grey space where I can pin up pictures and poke my head over the partition whenever I want some social interaction in what is called 'prairie dogging'. But the cubicle walls are made of fabric, and they're not a very effective barrier to noise.

Many of my colleagues like to play music while they work and at times there are several different songs playing at the same time. The cubicle walls do not help and I find it difficult to concentrate on the articles I'm reading when all I can hear is 'Shake Your Money Maker'.

It's not that I don't like music. But I don't like it inflicted on me at 120 decibels when I'm trying to work. The problem is that it doesn't sound that loud or irritating to most people. But to me it feels as if I'm walking around with no clothes on, without any skin, all my nerve endings exposed and quivering, and picking up every tremulous wave of sound, every puff of air, every whisper, while everyone else is in fur coats. People wonder what I'm complaining about because I look 'normal'. If they could see my sensitivity, maybe they'd turn the music down.

Eventually I graduate to my own office. But then everything changes. Someone decides that open-plan offices are good for team-building, office morale and communication. In other words, they suit people who love to socialize, who get their energy from being around others and can't get enough witty banter, small talk and chitchat. For introverts and HSPs like myself, they are a turn towards the dark side.

I know a lot of non-sensitive people like a bit of background noise in the form of the hum of human voices. It helps them to concentrate and makes them feel that they're part of something. But I just can't get used to it. I can't block it out. I can hear my computer humming, the photocopier roaring and the heating system droning. Doors are slamming, phones are ringing, people are talking. I can hear their fingers tapping on their keyboards. Someone drops a book on a desk and it lands with a thwack! Ladies in high-heeled shoes stomp down the thinly carpeted halls like soldiers in combat boots.

I can see the distant rays of sunlight through the rows of sealed windows while the fluorescent lights hum overhead. The ventilation system blows cold drafts down the back of my neck. My frozen fingers hover over the keyboard. I can smell coffee and perfume, chewing gum and oranges, the unnerving, decaying odour of old dust burning on a radiator. There's a great human symphony of fidgeting, scratching, sniffing, coughing, sneezing, nail biting, nose blowing and paper rustling that goes on all day. And I can feel the intangible, undeniable, nerve-shattering waves of other people's energy washing over me and soaking into my skin.

I can tell that the person sitting closest to me is upset. She hasn't said anything, but I can feel it. Someone else is stressed out. Another person is worrying about her kids. My boss is worried that she's not doing a good job. I can feel all of it and I wonder what I should do. I don't say anything. I know I will be accused of complaining or being too demanding when all I want is to help people feel better.

I turn on my computer. I have 300 emails. I'm a creative, ideas-oriented person, so I find this deluge of information rather overwhelming. But I start working my way through the messages, answering questions, fulfilling requests, pushing my projects onward, sorting out messes. I spend the next eight hours attending to administrative tasks, endless demands and dozens of simultaneous project schedules. There is no creativity, no idea generation, no opportunity to do anything meaningful. The enormous volume of detail leaves me feeling rattled, so I need to take a break and be alone, just for a few minutes. But in this environment, there is nowhere to go. Even the kitchen is crammed with people making tea and coffee, chatting, catching up, gossiping, all in one tiny windowless room. There are even tables in there for meetings, which is something like negotiating a peace treaty at Heathrow Airport.

I take a break and make my way to the ladies' room. I go into a stall, lock the door behind me and sit down. My mouth is dry. My heart is pounding. I lift my shaking hands to my face. I feel the heat rise into my cheeks as I begin to cry. I blow my nose and wipe my tears as I hear the bathroom door open as voices laugh and skate around the whitewashed walls. I take a deep breath and straighten my jacket. Time to go back to work.

Making sense of sensitivity

The world of work is a challenge for an HSP. The physical working environment is often stressful and overstimulating for highly sensitive senses. Bright lights, lots of noise, too many people and lack of time alone can make even a good job a difficult experience.

At the same time, deadlines, demands, gossip, competition and a focus on profits can drain the spirit out of highly sensitive people. We fear becoming 'institutionalized': working in a concrete building at a meaningless job among hundreds of others can be soul-destroying and can make you feel like just a grain of sand on a beach, rather than a person with unique skills and something valuable to contribute.

Highly sensitive people are curious, intuitive and insightful, and question things in our search for truth. We're highly creative and have an active imagination, so we're always coming up with new ideas. But it can be hard for an HSP to receive criticism or negative feedback, because we care so much about our work.

We can become perfectionists. We set high standards for ourselves and we don't want to let ourselves or anyone else down. Our generally quiet, soft-spoken and introverted nature also means that we're unlikely to express our concerns when environmental issues bother us at work.

Highly sensitive people tend to be meticulous, conscientious, reliable and hardworking, but these quiet and studious work habits mean that we're often overlooked for recognition and promotion in favour of more assertive and outspoken colleagues.

When our skills, talents and traits go unnoticed and we feel unappreciated, we can become emotionally detached from our work, making it even less meaningful and more stressful. Researchers (Evers et al. 2008) found that highly sensitive people can feel overwhelmed by working environments, and by work that is unmanageable and meaningless. Highly sensitive people can also develop a sense of alienation that stops them from reaching their true potential. Our frustration associated with work and our seeming inability to change or influence things can also lead us to feeling stressed, depressed or bad about ourselves.

The popular focus on teamwork, group projects and collaboration doesn't fit with the HSP sense of individuality or our artistic nature either. It can make us feel stifled and curtail our freedom of expression and our ability to think of possibilities. We prefer to work alone and often do our best work when left to our own devices. We're good at noticing subtle distinctions and details, while also focusing on the big picture, and we're able to concentrate deeply, which makes us excellent at taking on big projects.

Most highly sensitive people don't perform well when being observed, and we don't like to be rushed. We observe what's happening around us and we need time to process, reflect and develop ideas and solutions. Most workplaces simply don't offer or encourage that way of thinking.

People have often told me 'You think too much' and 'You're always overanalyzing'. I used to take this to heart and feel bad about myself. I assumed they were right, that there was something I was doing that was just wrong and unacceptable. But I don't feel that way anymore. I don't believe I think too much. I just like to think. It's what Elaine Aron refers to as 'depth of processing' and is the most fundamental aspect of high sensitivity.

Some researchers have suggested that there is a connection between high sensitivity and giftedness. Giftedness is hard to define. Many experts believe it's more than just about intelligence. In her 1999 book, *The Gifted Adult*, Mary-Elaine Jacobsen describes the following as some of the traits of gifted adults:

- Insatiable curiosity
- Ability to learn rapidly
- Less motivated than others by rewards, bonuses and praise
- Comfortable with a wide range of emotions
- Value honesty, integrity and ethics
- Ability to help others understand themselves better
- Sensitive to the slightest changes in the environment
- Driven
- A sense of wonder

These characteristics certainly sound a lot like those associated with high sensitivity. The psychologist and psychiatrist Kazimierz Dabrowski (1967) also made a connection between gifted people and sensitivity. While studying gifted children, he noticed that they displayed higher levels of excitability in five key areas, which sound like HSP traits: excess of energy, either physically or mentally; heightened sensory awareness; vivid imagination; passionate about knowledge; and highly emotional. He believed these excitabilities to be caused by greater than average sensitivity and that they enabled certain individuals to excel in learning and at work.

But Elaine Aron (2004) says that not all gifted people are highly sensitive and not all HSPs are gifted. She also suggests that HSP shyness, depression, anxiety or low self-esteem might have prevented us from identifying ourselves or being recognized as a gifted person. We may not have expressed our true skills and talents because we felt so unaccepted as sensitive people. We may have unwittingly used our natural compassion and empathy to please others and gain acceptance instead of using those skills for our own personal development.

Clearly, highly sensitive people need more than just a pay cheque. We need to be more than just a cog in the machine.

We need to know that we're doing something meaningful and that our work is helping others in some way. We also have an intense interest in moral issues – when we see injustice we want to do something about it and we're not afraid to stand up for our beliefs. We're often drawn to creative fields like art, music and writing, or to helping professions like counselling or therapy. It's not enough for us to just do the job. We need to feel that our work makes a difference.

Unfortunately, these kinds of jobs are often very hard to find. They don't often pay well, and we struggle to make a living. So we end up trying to make ourselves fit into an uncomfortable role or situation, where we inevitably feel unsatisfied, frustrated, stressed and unfulfilled. Alternatively, we take on less stressful positions to protect our sensitivities, but our skills, talents and drives remain unappreciated and unused. In either case, the lack of meaning in these occupations, coupled with long hours, an overstimulating workplace and the demands of the job usually leave us too exhausted to do anything at the end of the day but recover.

For many highly sensitive people, just figuring out what we really want to do is the challenge. We might know that we feel unsatisfied with what we're doing, but we don't know what else to do or how to change it. We know what we don't want, but we don't have any idea of what our true calling really is. Because meaningful work is so important to highly sensitive people, this lack of focus can easily lead us to feeling anxious, depressed, stressed, insecure and vulnerable to illness.

Highly sensitive people absorb a lot of information and we think deeply about it, processing, analysing, making connections and coming up with new ideas. Unfortunately, it's hard for others to know what's happening inside our minds. When we pause before acting or speaking, or we need time to reflect, non-HSPs can assume we're not thinking at all. In our extravert-centred world, if we're not saying anything, it appears as though we're not doing anything. But instead of trying to suppress our sensitivity, we need to embrace it. And we need to find a career that will let us use it.

What I learned

Finding a comfortable balance between supporting yourself financially and cherishing yourself personally comes down to knowing and valuing your unique traits. Here's what I have learned about working as an HSP.

1 **Create the working life you want.** Most corporate jobs are not suited to an HSP. While it's hard to find a balance between making a living and being true to who you are, don't try to squeeze yourself into a traditional work role if it doesn't feel right. In many of my jobs, I enjoyed the kind of work I was doing, but I often felt that I was living someone else's life. Working in a big city, in a busy office full of people, with tight deadlines and lots of multitasking just exhausted me.

   Instead, carve out a role that fits you. Don't settle for something you don't really enjoy just because it's a steady job or your parents have told you to do it. Fortunately, more and more companies are offering flexible working hours, so if you love your job but can't stand the office environment, you might be able to work at home, work non-standard hours or find a quiet space in the office so that you can control your stress levels and still find time for creative pursuits. Sometimes, all you need to do is ask for what you want. And then you'll not only be making a living, but creating a life worth living.

2 **Find work that matches your personality.** The key to a happy working life is finding work that suits your personality and temperament. The more you understand yourself, who you are, what you want and what you need, the easier it will be to focus on your goals and head confidently in the right direction. It's lack of direction that keeps you wandering from one unsatisfying experience to another. Many HSPs, for example, dislike administrative work but love to learn and prefer to work alone at their own pace, with minimal distractions and an opportunity for creative and/or intuitive expression.

   Finding a career that will allow you to work with your natural preferences, rather than fighting against them, is crucial. Start by discovering who you really are. The Myers-Briggs Type Indicator® is a questionnaire created by Katherine Myers and Isabel Briggs that measures individual differences. Their work is based on the book *Psychological Types* by Carl Jung. I also highly recommend the book *Please Understand Me*, by David Keirsey, for further understanding of your personality type, including insights into individual career preferences.

All highly sensitive people need to do the kind of work that has meaning, but there is no one perfect job for all highly sensitive people. What feels right for you depends on your own skills, personality and interests. But most of us want to do something that helps other people or uses our creativity, or both. It's only when you work in jobs where you can't use your natural abilities that high sensitivity feels like a curse. When you can use your natural HSP traits, such as empathy, compassion and deep processing, your sensitivity becomes an asset and a joy.

3 **Work towards your calling.** Highly sensitive people need more than just a job. We need to feel valued and appreciated and we need our work to be meaningful. We need to have a purpose. Of course, this makes finding the ideal career even more challenging. But when we do find it, our lives become richer, fuller and deeply fulfilling because we know that our work matters. When you spend time doing things that express who you really are, with all your unique skills and abilities, it doesn't even feel like work. It feels like you're putting something beautiful into the world that will benefit others.

If you break your long-term goal down into smaller steps, it won't seem so daunting. Hemingway wrote about writing a novel, 'All you have to do is write one true sentence. Once I did that, I could go on from there.' You don't have to write a whole novel, start your own business or change the world today; just write one true sentence. Just take one step. But take it.

4 **Use your sensitivity to help others.** Because we are so in tune with other people's emotions, it's natural for highly sensitive people to enjoy helping professions. Many highly sensitive people enjoy working as a counsellor or therapist. They find the one-to-one of counselling, mentoring, tutoring or therapy work allows them to use their empathy, compassion, awareness and depth of processing in a way that helps others, which is deeply fulfilling. I found I could use all my HSP drives and skills, while helping people and being creative at the same time by writing articles, books and blog posts.

Elaine Aron (1996) calls HSPs 'priestly advisors'. In a world where most people are what Aron calls 'warrior kings', the action-oriented, dominance-seeking non-HSPs, highly sensitive people are in the minority. Instead of leading with force and power, and conquering the world, we're the advisors and thinkers. We're here to teach, heal, shape the laws of society, and observe the laws of nature. We're the wise men and women who want to develop our understanding of the world and share it with others through our work, our nature and the way we live our lives.

If you are an HSP who does work with other people, you need to maintain strong and clear boundaries so that you don't get drawn too deeply into the lives of others or give too much of yourself. The best way to help someone else is by being an example of integrity. Be yourself and when you see someone struggling, throw them a rope. You don't have to jump into the sea with them.

5 **Use your sensitivity to be creative.** There is a strong connection between high sensitivity and creativity, according to Elaine Aron and creativity coach Lisa Riley (2015). Being highly sensitive means that we are open to experiences, and have the imagination to dream up new ideas and create fresh innovations. For many HSPs, the ideal career involves some kind of creativity, whether that's art, music, writing, dance or theatre. Creativity is one of the assets of being a highly sensitive person, so use your creative mind to come up with possibilities for the way you want to work.

6 **Become self-employed.** For many HSPs, this is the answer to the world of work. When you are your own boss, you can control your hours, your working environment, the people you work with and the kind of work you do. Highly sensitive people are ideally suited to entrepreneurship because we possess the traits needed for such an endeavour – we're conscientious, hardworking, self-motivated, curious, careful, dedicated, full of ideas and passionate about our work. But being self-employed brings its own risks as well. As your own boss, you are responsible for the success of your business and HSPs might find themselves working long hours, worrying excessively and becoming exhausted.

7 **Don't be a victim.** It's easy for highly sensitive people to become trapped in a victim role, even when it comes to work and the way

we spend our spare time. We struggle to find jobs that will fulfil us in a world more focused on monetary gain. We try to develop a sense of camaraderie with co-workers in office environments that leave us overwhelmed. And we strive to find a connection to our community in an age of electronic communication. Ultimately, we're often left feeling that life is a series of struggles that we are constantly trying to cope with.

When we find ourselves unhappy about our situation, we feel worn out and frustrated, and we feel stuck. In this mindset, we can set ourselves up to become victims of our circumstances, forcing ourselves to settle for whatever comes along, and for whatever happens. But while our natural instinct is to retreat to regain our strength, a proactive approach can be the secret to our success. Don't wait for the right career to come to you. Figure out who you are and what you really want to do and, in the words of Henry David Thoreau, 'Go confidently in the direction of your dreams. Live the life you've imagined.'

8 **Take what you need.** Whatever kind of work you choose to do, take the time and space you need to do the things you enjoy. Take time to think and write down your thoughts and feelings and get to know yourself. And take the initiative to create a career without criticism, contempt or attempts to stifle your sensitivity. Find a job that feeds your soul and a working environment that gives you peace. And it you can't find one, create the work you need. Remember, the world needs the gifts you have to offer. And you need a chance to let your imagination run free.

10
Nature and animals

'Nature never did betray the heart that loved her.'

William Wordsworth

I'm at my parents' house, sitting outside on their garden swing. My dog Bandit is lying in the grass nearby. He's a big black Labrador/ Doberman cross who looks like a guard dog but wouldn't hurt a fly. I adopted him from the RSPCA shelter when he was eight years old, which is near middle age for dogs, but we soon became close friends.

I've just received a phone call from my boyfriend, telling me that our relationship is over. Sitting on the garden swing, I start to cry. Bandit gets up and climbs on to the swing next to me. And then he looks up at me and puts his paw on my knee. He knows how I feel. I'm sure he can feel it and he feels sad for me. It is the most beautiful and touching expression of compassion I've ever experienced.

A year later, I'm living in Faringdon, a small market town about 18 miles southwest of Oxford on the edge of the Cotswolds. One of the reasons I moved from Canada to England, ironically, was that I felt I needed more space. There is a lot of land in Canada, but there aren't a lot of public footpaths. There aren't any walkers' rights of way. When I first came to England and saw the public footpath signs everywhere, I thought I'd found heaven.

I'm working in a large, multi-storey office building, the kind with windows that don't open. Outside, there are trees and small, park-like spaces, a post office, a shop, a café and even a hairdresser. It's all engineered to create a little community. Inside, I can sit at my desk and look out across a sea of people stretching all the way to the other side of the building. There must be about two hundred people on my floor. But despite being surrounded by people, I feel a terrible sense of isolation, a complete lack of connection or intimacy.

I've bought myself a guide to walking trails in the Cotswolds, so one weekend in May, I drive out to a pretty old town in the area called Winchcombe. With my map and guidebook, my hiking boots on, and a bottle of water in my backpack, I set off along the lane, heading out of the town and into the forests and green rolling hills of the countryside. I feel more relaxed already as I notice the sunlight slipping through the trees, the sudden scent of a lavender bush, and the curious stares of the cows as I walk through their field.

I'm walking along a path when I stop, struck by the beauty of a bird on a branch and a cool, green tunnel created by overgrown leaves. I pull out my camera and take a picture, capturing the moment.

Along the way, I pass Hailes Abbey, a Cistercian abbey founded in 1246, later dissolved by Henry VIII in 1539 and now a ghostly ruin of stones and shadows amid the rising grass. Further on, after a series of gates and stiles and woodland paths, the lane begins to climb on a broad track and curves around a gathering of trees and bushes.

I'm listening to music on my iPod, a mix of Vaughan Williams, Bach and Vivaldi. As I reach the top of the hill and follow the path around a bend, the magnificent view of the sloping green landscape and the church tower of Winchcombe appears in the distance. At that moment, I'm listening to Vivaldi's Gloria, stepping along an ancient pathway with nothing around me but the majesty and the glory of the natural world.

In this moment, I feel what I can only describe as euphoric bliss. The beauty of nature, the peace and quiet, and the music have given me a feeling of joy I fear others might only dream of. This deep appreciation and love of nature and the arts is one of the blessings of being a highly sensitive person.

In a way, it's the kind of feeling, that sense of peace, inner calm and joyousness that people often use to describe their faith. This is what we're supposed to feel when we're in church. I have never felt that way about religion, but I feel it here. I feel it every time I go for a walk in the natural world. This is where truth and beauty live. This is the source of peace and connection, here, out in the wide open spaces of the countryside, on the hills, in the sea, in the still, silent moments of the bluebell woods. This is my cathedral.

Making sense of sensitivity

Research (Mayer et al. 2009) shows that nature can improve our health and wellbeing. It increases relaxation, reduces stress and improves our mood. Walking in nature for just 15 minutes increases our positive feelings, our ability to concentrate and our ability to reflect on a problem. Scientists (Davis 2004) have also discovered that nature helps us to recover faster from a stressful event. Even looking at pictures or a video of nature helps individuals recover faster from stress.

Just being outside makes people feel more energetic, according to a series of studies (Ryan et al. 2010). And these findings show that it's not exercise or socializing with other people that provide the benefits of getting out of the house. Just being outdoors makes us feel better. Earlier research (Weinstein et al. 2009) also showed that people actually become more caring and generous when they spend time in nature. This might be because it relaxes us and helps us to slow down and take the time to reflect.

Nature relaxes us because of what psychologists call 'attention restoration theory' (ART) (Kaplan 1995). Essentially, spending time in nature gives our brain a chance to rest. While woods and flowers, birds, rivers and trees are an engaging, sensory feast, research shows that the brain doesn't have to work to notice and appreciate them. They capture our attention and we enjoy them without effort, which gives us the opportunity to replenish and restore ourselves. Man-made surroundings, business meetings, traffic, email and urban environments, on the other hand, bombard us with stimuli that demand our attention, which is tiring for the brain.

But nature has an even more significant impact on highly sensitive people. We not only enjoy time spent in nature, we need it. Exposure to nature soothes our fragile nervous systems. Our constant exposure to stress, working in a fast-paced culture, coping with traffic, technology and city life means that a walk in the woods can feel like a warm bath after a hard day. Highly sensitive people need the gentle soothing that nature provides.

At the same time, our deep appreciation of nature and beauty and our intense awareness of our environment create a powerful connection between ourselves and the natural world. Nature is a balm for our sensitive souls and we find ourselves seeking it out, drawn to its quiet, gentle presence where we can slow down, reflect and breathe. It's where we can at last be ourselves. And consequently, we are liberated and moved by it in a way that others can only imagine.

In some ways, high sensitivity is like mindfulness. Studies (Howell et al. 2011) have shown that spending time in nature makes people more aware of the present moment, a key part of mindfulness as well as high sensitivity. Other research (Aspinall et al. 2015) suggests that walking through green spaces can put the brain into a meditative state, allowing you to pay attention to the world around you, while creating the calmness needed for reflection. It's in this calm, quiet reflective state that creativity can flourish.

In further research (Davis 2004), scientists suggest that nature can also stimulate 'peak experiences'. These are optimal states of mind in which a person feels euphoria, a sense of beauty, love and harmony with the universe. This is certainly what I felt that day in the Cotswolds.

Highly sensitive people are aware of our surroundings and the people in it, and we absorb the energy of those people and both the man-made and natural worlds. Taking time to stop and appreciate the beauty all around us is what mindfulness teaches. I believe it's what highly sensitive people do naturally.

Highly sensitive people also have a connection with animals. According to Elaine Aron (2007), highly sensitive people seem to understand them better than other people because we notice their non-verbal communication with us. To understand animals, you need to be patient, quiet, gentle and pay attention, all common HSP qualities. I've also had a lot of positive experiences with animals. I feel connected to them but, even more surprisingly, they seem to know that I understand them. Dogs and cats have stopped in their tracks when I walk by and they look at me, as if they recognize me as one of their own, a fellow sensitive. On my walks in the country, horses and other people's dogs will approach me and sometimes follow me, leaving their owners behind. Studies (McConnell 2011) show that pet owners report less depression and anxiety, higher self-esteem and an ability to cope better with grief and stress.

Like most highly sensitive people, I care so much about animals that I find any kind of animal mistreatment unbearable. I cry at animal shelter commercials on TV. I have to change the channel. Seeing animals mistreated is incredibly upsetting. I can't bear to see them suffer any more than I can bear to see people suffer. It feels like more than compassion. It's more than just understanding or imagining what they're going through. I can feel what they're feeling. When a child cries or a dog yelps, I know they're suffering. I can feel it. And it leaves me in tears every time.

What I learned

The increasing use of technology means that many of us are spending nearly all our lives indoors and in front of a screen. And while everyone can benefit from time spent in nature, highly sensitive people depend on it. Highly sensitive people are as sensitive as animals, and our connection to nature is what gives us strength. Here are a few more things I've learned about the natural world and being an HSP.

1 **Spend time in nature.** Whether it's gardening, walking in a park, swimming in the sea or hiking in the mountains, make time in the natural world a priority. I actually moved countries because, ironically, it was easier for me to go for regular walks in the country in England than in Canada. The UK has created an environment for walkers, with guidebooks, well-maintained paths, public rights of way, clear signposts and walking clubs. So I get out there every weekend and give my sensitive brain the rest it needs. I also try to get outside for shorter walks in my local park, avoiding the busy streets whenever I can.

   When I was living on Vancouver Island, I went for a swim in the ocean every day in the summer. There is something magically healing about water. If I was feeling sad, frustrated or unhappy, then I'd emerge from the ocean feeling cleansed and restored, as if the sea had washed my sadness away. Walks in the woods, strolls on the beach, and swimming in that great big sea supported me, renewed me and gave me the strength to move forward with a sense of peace. Nature gave me back myself.

2 **Avoid big cities.** I've found that whenever I live in a city, I constantly feel rattled. There's just too much stimulation going on

for a highly sensitive person. I used to live and work in Toronto, taking the subway and the streetcar to work. By the time I got home, I'd be shaking and exhausted, just from the commute. There were just too many people, too much noise, too many cars and buses and billboards for my mind to absorb. Cities leave me saturated.

Most jobs are located in big cities, so they can be difficult to avoid, but I've tried to live in smaller places or on the edge of a city. I'm fortunate enough to have a car, so I also like to drive instead of taking public transport because it's quieter, and buses and trains are often packed full of the energy of other people, especially at rush hour. In my car, I'm in a little steel bubble, protected from the noise of the outside world. But I do care about the environment, so I carpool with friends when possible and when I take the bus or train, I always wear my earphones so I can listen to music. I also try to plan the journey ahead of time so I don't get frazzled wondering where I'm going. I find that even suburbs can be quite overwhelmingly noisy. As fun and convenient as it is to live in the city, your highly sensitive nervous system will pay the price.

3 **Get a pet.** Animals can make us physically healthier. They lower our blood pressure and boost our immune system. Walking a dog gets us outside for walks in the fresh air on a regular basis. And they also lift our spirits and help us relax. Owning a pet is a wonderful way to give back for all the love they've given you. When you give them a safe, comfortable home with plenty of food, water and affection, they know you care about them. If you adopt a pet from a shelter, they seem to know that you've rescued them and they will be your loyal friend for life.

4 **Walk solo.** Walking groups can be a great way to meet new people and socialize in the outdoors, but they can also be draining for highly sensitive people. The benefits of spending time in nature come from savouring the experience and giving your mind a chance to rest. That means enjoying and noticing your surroundings, the colour of the leaves, the scent of the flowers, the sound of a babbling brook. When I walk with a group, these things become buried beneath the conversation and laughter, especially when there are a lot of people. I've joined walking groups and met some nice people, but at the

end of the walk, I sometimes feel stressed from the stimulation of socializing.

Being an HSP, I also tend to find myself in the role of compassionate listener, trapped in a five-mile walk while someone unloads. I think that, because highly sensitive people are generally empathic and caring, we seem to attract people who want someone to listen to them. And while it can make us feel good to be a comfort to others, it can also be a burden. We can easily be taken advantage of by people who simply want to unleash their frustrations, thoughts and emotions on to us. Consequently, we absorb their feelings and can quickly become overwhelmed.

Highly sensitive people need time in nature to replenish their depleted resources. We absorb more information than other people, so we need more time in the natural world to replenish our own energy reserves and give our sensitive selves a chance to rest and recuperate from the daily onslaught of stress and stimulation. Walking on your own can give you the opportunity to relax and recharge and get back to being your sensitive self.

5 **Use nature to soothe your shattered soul.** What I've learned in my life is that some experiences feel too much to bear. But when you feel overwhelmed, nature is often what your mind, body and soul need more than anything else. And nature won't ever let you down. Whenever I've felt sad, lonely, depressed or upset, a walk in the woods, away from the chaos of modern life and the draining energy of other people, is like a soothing balm for my sensitive self. The feeling is so tangible, it's like a drug that calms you down and lifts you up. It lets you breathe again.

When you stop battling the stresses and strains that keep you locked in a fight for your own survival, you can see the beauty that's all around you, the wondrous loveliness that blooms in nature's wide open spaces and quiet corners. And while nature calms your rattled nerves, that beauty begins to fill the emptiness inside you. The beauty of nature and animals fills us up with hope and love, inspiration and energy, and the passion to unleash the creativity that simmers within all of us, just waiting to be let go.

11
Creativity

'The truly creative mind in any field is no more than this: A human creature born abnormally, inhumanly sensitive. To him... a touch is a blow, a sound is a noise, a misfortune is a tragedy, a joy is an ecstasy, a friend is a lover, a lover is a god, and failure is death. Add to this cruelly delicate organism the overpowering necessity to create, create, create – so that without the creating of music or poetry or books or buildings or something of meaning, his very breath is cut off from him. He must create, must pour out creation. By some strange, unknown, inward urgency he is not really alive unless he is creating.'

Pearl S. Buck

I'm in the second grade, about eight years old, and living in London, Ontario. My teacher has pasted construction paper flowers across the back wall of our classroom. But they are just green stems and leaves. We have to add the petals, she tells us, by writing a poem or a story. We will receive one petal for each to stick on our flower. My best friend is determined to have the most petals in the whole class. To her, it's a competition and she has to win. So every day after school we go to her house and start writing poems.

I kneel on the green carpet of her bedroom, my elbows perched on her bed and my pen and notepad lying in wait. My friend is sitting on the floor on the other side of the bed. She has a pen and a notepad as well. She ducks under the bed for a moment and then reappears with an armload of books that she spreads across the bed. There are so many, I can hardly see the pattern of the bedspread anymore.

She flips one open, flattening the page with one hand and taking up her pen with the other.

'What are you doing?' I ask.

'I'm writing a poem,' she says. 'I've got so many poetry books here, I'll get all the petals. It'll be easy.'

'Oh. You're copying a poem from a book?' I ask.

'Yeah. It's much faster than thinking one up yourself.'

'That's a good idea.'

'Here,' she tosses me a book. 'Have one. I've got lots.'

She is so smart. She is a straight-A student and she has already decided where she will go to university. I don't think I'm very smart. I'm certainly not clever enough to think of using poems from books.

But I'm not interested in winning contests or being the best. I don't think I could. And I don't want to have more petals than anyone else. I want to have good petals, quality petals, petals that mean something. So instead of copying a poem out of a book, I start to write my own.

The next day, we go back to my friend's house and she spreads her poetry books across her bed again. This time, I decide to write a short story about the first time I went ice skating on the frozen pond in the field behind our house one cold, grey winter. My parents didn't know how to skate, so they stood there in the snow, watching me and my sister as we wobbled and stumbled around the pond. I was not very elegant, but I managed to stay upright. A few years later, they built houses on that field and filled in the pond. I would watch their timber frames slowly rising up from the ground as I walked to school. I never went ice skating again.

By the end of the school year, the entire back wall of our classroom is covered in yellow paper petals. There are so many, it's hard to tell whose flower was whose. But you can see that some flowers have only a few petals and some don't have any. My friend's flower is a big, sprawling botanical that has somehow blossomed in our Canadian winter, spreading its petals across the wall and up to the ceiling like a vine.

When our teacher announces the winner, I'm not surprised. My friend has the most petals of anyone in the class. She's awarded first prize, which ironically is a book of poetry. I'm proud of her, even though I know by this point that she cheated.

But to my surprise, I am awarded second place. When my teacher announces my name, I walk shyly up to the front of the classroom and collect my prize. It's a notebook. On the cover, there's a photograph of a skier flying through the air in a mist of snowy powder and a hazy orange sunset. I like the colour of the tangerine sky and the bittersweet hope of that apricot sun.

I walk quickly back to my desk amid the thundering applause and sit down. I open the notebook. Inside the front cover, my teacher has written a note: 'Congratulations on winning second place in the writing contest, in the hopes that you will write many more excellent stories.'

I know then that I want to write. I knew as soon as I wrote my first poem on my friend's bed. And I know that writing stories that are honest and real means something important. It means more to me than medals or trophies. I just know there are thoughts and feelings, stories and ideas inside me that are bursting to get out. I don't know if anyone else wants them, but I know I can't keep them buried. I just know that writing makes me feel like the skier on the cover of my notebook, flying through the air in a perfect sunlit moment, capturing beauty, even if there's no one there to see it.

Making sense of sensitivity

Highly sensitive people constantly absorb sensory information and energy, and we need a way to release it. Creative pursuits provide us with an outlet for that energy.

But creativity is not an act of draining yourself or giving your thoughts and ideas away. It's a process of filling yourself up, of filling that empty space inside you. When I write, I'm not left depleted and exhausted. I walk away with a feeling of fulfilment, wholeness, and the sense that I have everything I need.

Being creative is not about being a great artist or a famous composer. It's being open to experience, to thoughts and ideas, and possessing an insatiable curiosity to learn more. Creativity is the energy and enthusiasm for expressing ourselves without fear, the way children do. In this sense, high sensitivity allows us to maintain our creativity. Children are creative by nature, but the realities of life, including the criticism and judgment we receive, mean that most people grow out of their creativity, suppress it or forget how to be creative. Sensitive people don't. High sensitivity is a trait that allows us to retain our creativity, our active imaginations, and our curiosity, enthusiasm and sense of wonder.

My creativity has always been there for me. It never lets me down. Even when everything else in life is going wrong, when people disappoint me, when things don't go as planned, I can sit down at my desk and find it. Sometimes it takes a while. Creativity can't be rushed. But when you take a deep breath and let yourself relax, creativity emerges, like a dolphin out of a still blue sea. You can't always see it, but it's always there, waiting for life to be calm enough to come to the surface.

Being creative also helps us to connect with others by sharing our ideas through works of art. In their book *Wired to Create: Unravelling the Mysteries of the Creative Mind*, psychologist Scott Barry Kaufman and writer Carolyn Gregoire cite a study of musicians. These artists described music as a way to express themselves while connecting with others, saying that art was a way of bridging their inner and outer worlds. When we write, draw, paint, take photos or make music, we are helping people understand who we are. We're also getting in touch with emotions and experiences so personal, but so universal, that we can begin to understand others. That sense of being understood, of letting people see themselves in a poem or a painting, is one of the ways that highly sensitive people can really touch people's lives. When we use our creativity, we can help people, just by being ourselves.

Are highly sensitive people more creative?

Elaine Aron believes that all highly sensitive people are creative, although it's not clear whether all creative people are highly sensitive.

A study in the *Journal of Personality and Social Psychology* (Carson 2013) revealed that creative people's brains tend to be more open to environmental stimuli, a key characteristic of highly sensitive people. In a process called 'latent inhibition', most people unconsciously block out information that they don't need. But the researchers found that creative people, like HSPs, have low levels of latent inhibition, so they absorb more information.

According to psychologist Robert Alan Black, author of *Broken Crayons*, being sensitive helps us to be more creative in a number of ways. We're more aware of problems, we can sense what's happening around us and we care, all of which contribute to creativity. In 1980 Black developed a list of 32 traits of creative people, which he then combined with Dr E. Paul Torrance's 20 measurable characteristics of creativity to create a comprehensive list of traits of creative people, including curiosity, idealism, imagination and the ability to sense emotions in others. Many of these qualities also describe highly sensitive people.

Psychologist Mihaly Csikszentmihalyi, author of *Creativity: Flow and the Psychology of Discovery and Invention*, notes that creative people possess many contradictory qualities that make them unique. I've noticed that I have a lot of these contradictions in my own personality and I believe that many of the paradoxes that define a creative person can also apply to highly sensitive people. Here are some of the qualities Csikszentmihalyi (1996) has discovered in creative types:

1 Creative people have a lot of energy, but they also need lots of rest. Downtime gives them the opportunity to recharge so they can focus their energy and concentrate on activities that matter to them.
2 They tend to be both smart and naive, both wise and childlike. This paradox enables creative people to use both convergent and divergent thinking, that is, using logic to solve problems and recognize good ideas, while also being open-minded enough to be able to develop new concepts.
3 They combine playfulness with the discipline and perseverance needed to put their ideas into a piece of work. Creative people know that, along with the fun of imagination, successful creativity requires the dedication and drive of hard work.

Being creative gives me a deep sense of connection, a sense of satisfaction that I can't often find elsewhere. It gives me a rootedness to who I really am. And being true to myself and doing what I really like to do gives me a sense of peace.

Doing the work that expresses your true nature gives you a feeling that you are not even working at all because you experience what can only be described as bliss. Similarly, as Csikszentmihalyi notes, not working at your speciality, not doing anything creative, can leave you feeling utterly empty and without purpose.

What stops us being creative?

If highly sensitive people are naturally creative, what prevents us from expressing our creativity?

Because highly sensitive people absorb so much information from the environment, we can easily become saturated and overwhelmed, which drains our energy. As empathic and compassionate people, highly sensitive people also tend to give a lot of time and energy to helping others. We need lots of downtime to regain our strength and restore our creative resources. Creativity is a natural expression of our thoughts and feelings, but it takes energy to create. And when we feel we have nothing left to give, our creative well can run dry.

In her book, *Mindset: The New Psychology of Success*, psychologist Carol Dweck suggests that most of us think that we're either born with talent and intelligence or we're not. But Dweck says it's your mindset, or the way you think about things, that determines whether or not you'll act on your abilities and become successful.

Most of us grow up with what she calls a fixed mindset, which means that we believe our personalities, talents and intelligence are set in stone at birth. When we think this way, however, any criticism of our creative efforts feels like a personal attack. Our creative work is a representation of ourselves, and criticism of that can be painful. We feel rejected, disappointed in ourselves, and believe that there's no point in trying again because we cannot change. We believe that we only have limited amounts of skill or talent and they're just not good enough.

This fear of being judged often stops us from acting on our creativity or even expressing ourselves. Many HSPs have low self-esteem because of the criticism we've received just for being who we are, and so the thought of putting ourselves into the world with a work of art and subjecting ourselves to more criticism is more than we can bear. Putting your work into the public domain exposes you to potential criticism, ridicule or misunderstanding, which can be devastating to a sensitive soul. Being sensitive means that we are often highly expressive, but also fragile. And so we give up and stick to what we know we can do well so we can feel good about ourselves. But in the process, we abandon our creative selves and our potential.

Creativity is simply looking at things in a new way and seeing the possibilities. You can be creative when you write a story, take a photograph, cook, garden, start your own business, solve problems and take care of your children. It's doing what's meaningful to you that matters.

What I learned

Being creative isn't something that you can turn on and off like a light switch. It's always there inside you, but it needs to be nurtured. The first step is recognizing that you have something worth expressing. Here are a few other things I've learned.

1 **Develop a growth mindset.** When I was a child, I thought I was not clever, not talented, and certainly not a real writer. But my own life experience has shown me that none of that is true. And I came to that realization just by trying and making an effort. I read, studied and wrote, and the more I did, the more skilled I became. I don't need to have the most petals. I just need my petals to be genuine pieces of me.

   Being creative requires the belief that accomplishment isn't for the gifted few, according to *Mindset* author Carol Dweck. It's for anyone who takes the time and effort to practise and persevere. When you choose to shift from a fixed mindset to a growth mindset, you are giving yourself permission to make mistakes, fail and try again and that's how we learn and grow.

   We may not all become another Mozart or Einstein, but we all have enormous potential. Even geniuses aren't born perfect. They studied, struggled, tried, failed and kept trying. Dr Seuss's first book was rejected 27 times. The high school yearbook committee refused to accept Peanuts creator Charles Schultz's cartoons. Steven Spielberg failed to gain acceptance to the University of Southern California School of Theater, Film and Television three times. And Oprah Winfrey got fired from her first job as a TV reporter because they told her she wasn't right for television. Despite their talent and intelligence, it was the drive to keep going that led to their success. And it was curiosity and passion that fuelled their ambition. These are the qualities of highly sensitive people.

2   **Focus on the moment.** Children are often creative because they're not afraid of being judged or criticized. They don't think about other things when they sit down to draw. They simply enjoy what they're doing in the moment. Mindfulness teaches us that we can find peace and happiness when we stop ruminating on the past and worrying about the future. Highly sensitive people are so aware of what's happening around us that we are always living in and appreciating the moment. It's only when life becomes too stressful and bombards us with too much stimulation that that moment becomes cluttered and our creativity is buried beneath the chaos.

I write simply because I like the way it makes me feel. There's no other reason. When I do something creative, I'm living in the moment, where there's no pressure, no stress, expectations or demands. Just peace. It creates what Csikszentmihalyi calls 'flow', that wonderful experience of losing track of time when you engage in activities that completely capture your attention.

Engaging in a creative pursuit gives me the opportunity to release stress and express all that information I've been absorbing and let it go. It lets me express my thoughts, feelings and ideas in a way that is uniquely me. The more I am creative, the more I feel grounded, centred and the more it makes me feel like myself.

While highly sensitive people may be naturally creative, it's not always easy. We've got so many thoughts, worries and fears running around in our heads that it can feel terrifying to start. As the writer Dorothy Parker said, 'I hate writing, but I love having written.'

To begin, turn off the thinking and worrying. Take some time out, find a quiet place, turn on music that relaxes you and just play. Leave judgment and criticism at the door. They're not allowed in here. This is the time for your sensitive mind to express itself.

3   **Ignore the criticism of your choices.** When I was growing up, I was told I was never going to make a living as a writer. And of course I believed it. I continued writing, but I kept it hidden, like some kind of shameful secret. I didn't tell anyone and for a long time I was too afraid to take writing classes or attend conferences. Many of us have grown up in a culture that emphasizes prosperity and material wealth and that you can't do that as an artist, so don't

bother. Eventually, as I kept writing, I felt that being true to myself as a highly sensitive, creative person was more important than anything else. I was even offered a job as a bank manager once and I turned it down. I would certainly have made a good living, but I would've been miserable and no doubt too exhausted and defeated to be creative in my spare time. Working creatively gives highly sensitive people a kind of happiness that others may not ever experience. And we do that kind of work for the pure enjoyment of the process rather than the rewards it may bring.

But while critical judgement of your life choices should be ignored, constructive criticism of your work needs to be embraced. Getting feedback on something you've created is scary and it can feel like a personal attack. But that's how we learn and how we improve. Without some critical appraisal of your work, you may be productive and persevering, but you might be making the same mistakes over and over again without knowing it. Art is subjective and it's very difficult to see the flaws in your own work. Part of the experience of being an artist is getting rejected, repeatedly. Just ask Steven Spielberg. So work hard, put only your best stuff out there and see what comes back. Accept the criticism, have a little cry, see where you can improve, then get back to work.

4   **Take a break.** While we need to work hard, keep trying and persevere, sometimes we can try too hard. Creativity needs to be nurtured, so if you try really hard to come up with a new innovation, write a song, draw a landscape or fix a problem, sometimes the ideas just don't come. Sometimes, the best solution is just to stop trying and take a break.

In *Wired to Create*, Kaufman revealed that one of the best ways to relax and stimulate your creativity is to take a shower. He found that people reported that they are more likely to get new ideas in the shower than at work. And that's probably because, in the shower, we are more relaxed.

But it doesn't have to be the bathroom where you go for a little creative inspiration. You just need to get up and get away from your desk and let go of the pressure to create. Give yourself a little break from your own demands to let your mind roam free – whether it's a walk around the block, a stroll on the beach or a country drive. I frequently get ideas and solutions in the shower, but also while doing the dishes, cooking, or just looking at the trees outside my window.

5 **Think of yourself as an artist.** To unlock the creativity inside us, we need to start thinking of ourselves as artists. I believe that most highly sensitive people are creative. Just as we limit ourselves by thinking of sensitivity as a weakness, we also curb our creative potential when we see ourselves as ungifted. In her book, *Daybook: The Journal of an Artist*, Anne Truitt writes that, to unblock the creative flow, you must submit to the role of artist. Despite her obvious talent and success, Truitt herself resisted the idea of calling herself an artist for many years because she didn't think she was good enough to be an artist. But then she realized that she couldn't grow as an artist until she could accept that she was one.

I didn't think of myself as a writer or an artist or even a creative person for a long time. Real writers were famous. They were serious. They certainly didn't wear pink or have a Wallace and Gromit screen saver, so I couldn't possibly be a writer. One day, I thought, I will grow up and then I'll be a real writer. And so I waited. But then a friend said to me, 'Maybe writers do wear pink. Maybe they're just ordinary people. Maybe writers look just like you.' It was then I began to see myself not as a quiet, shy, overly sensitive being who spent too much time alone, but as a creative person, a writer. An artist. And the more we are ourselves, the more of an artist we will become.

6 **Remember that a relaxed mind is a creative mind.** Creativity can't be rushed and it doesn't work well under stress. But that doesn't mean it's not there. Like sensitivity, creativity needs to be treated gently. When you take a deep breath, become calm and unhurried, creativity has a chance to emerge.

Highly sensitive people need time to think and reflect. We absorb so much information, including other people's stress, that quiet time is essential. And yet when we do have quiet time, we're often too frazzled and exhausted to do anything creative. There has to be a doorway from hectic modern life to the calm and peaceful place where we can create.

I cannot write when I've got too much on my mind or when I feel stressed or overwhelmed from too much activity. So I make relaxation a priority. I try to get enough sleep, avoid stressful people and situations, listen to relaxing music when I'm working and go for regular walks in nature.

A fellow HSP told me that he liked to practice tai chi in a park next to a river. Afterwards he could feel a surge of creative flow and began writing poetry and drawing. He couldn't quite understand what it was about the river that made him feel creative. But I think sensitive people need sensitive places. And when we are relaxed and surrounded by other sensitive elements, like art and nature, we feel free to let our feelings show and our poetry blossom.

And that's how the door opens – not by force, but with the strength of sensitivity.

Conclusion

Life as a highly sensitive person in a non-sensitive world isn't easy. But it is a gift. We need to be honest with ourselves and accept ourselves for who we are and embrace it, not hide it. Don't try to be someone you're not. Don't conceal your sensitivity. Be open about it, and express yourself so that you can live the life you want to live. You are the only person who can get your needs met. Look after your sensitive self, whether that means leaving a noisy party, asking for flexible working hours or letting go of a hurtful relationship.

A highly sensitive person is like a person turned inside out. Non-HSPs can wrap themselves with a tough outer coating of cool, calm indifference, giving the appearance of strength, while their vulnerability remains tucked away inside. As HSPs, we live with all our sensitivities and vulnerabilities exposed, our emotions laid bare, our nerve endings revealed, raw and writhing. And this leaves us open to judgment and criticism, taunts and torments, and unprotected from the self-centred motives of people who want to take advantage of our gentle and caring nature.

But living inside out also means that while our sensitivity is seen and exposed, our strength is on the inside. And that's why so many people misunderstand us. They cannot see our strength, only our sensitivity. And all too often, we cannot see it ourselves. We've spent so much time defending ourselves and trying to figure out who we are and how to be that we haven't learned how to just be ourselves. And the more we do, the better we'll be. The more you live your life in a way that supports, respects, protects, nurtures and celebrates your sensitivity, the stronger and happier you will be.

Sensitivity is not a weakness. It can appear that way to onlookers and it can certainly feel that way when you're struggling to cope with the overstimulation of life's busyness and your own self-doubt. But high sensitivity is not a condition to be overcome. It is a trait to be cherished. It is what gives you strength. It is strength.

Sensitivity gives us compassion and empathy, but we need to use these gifts wisely, for ourselves as well as others. It gives us awareness of our world, openness to ideas and acceptance of novelty. It gives us depth of thought and the creativity to dream up new possibilities. These are wonderful gifts. Perhaps best of all is our natural and unceasing ability to appreciate the beauty in everything, every day.

Highly sensitive people are not born insecure. It's not an inherent part of the trait. But we often develop low self-esteem and negative feelings about ourselves because of the way we are treated and the misunderstandings and judgments other people have about who we are, who we should be and how we should act. We can't change other people. But we can change the way we respond to them. We can give ourselves the respect of choosing how to respond. And we can choose to love, respect and show compassion to ourselves as well.

Criticism is just a coat that someone has thrown over your shoulders. But you don't have to wear it. You can choose to keep it wrapped around you because it feels safe and familiar. Or you can shrug it off. And just be you. When you give yourself the love and care you need and deserve, and recognize yourself as someone who is wired to wonder, your creative, compassionate, sensitive self will flourish.

References

Acevedo, B.P., Aron, E., Aron, A., Sangster, M.D., Collins, N. & Brown, L. (2014). 'The Highly Sensitive Brain: An FMRI Study of Sensory Processing Sensitivity and Response to Others' Emotions'. *Brain and Behavior*, 4(4).

American Institute of Stress (2012). 'Take a Deep Breath'. Retrieved 6 November 2016 from <www.stress.org/take-a-deep-breath/>

Aron, E. (1996). *The Highly Sensitive Person.* New York: Broadway Books.

Aron, E. (2001). *The Highly Sensitive Person in Love.* New York: Broadway Books.

Aron, E. (2004). *The Highly Sensitive Person* (blog) 'The Highly Sensitive Child (and Adults, Too): Is Sensitivity the Same as Being Gifted?' Retrieved 17 February 2019 from <www.hsperson.com/pages/3Nov04.htm>

Aron, E. (2007). *The Highly Sensitive Person* (blog) 'What HSPs Can Give and Get from Animals and Babies'. Retrieved 2 February 2019 from <www.hsperson.com/pages/2Feb07.htm>

Aron, E. (2012a). *The Highly Sensitive Person* (blog) 'HSPs and Fibromyalgia, Chronic Fatigue Syndrome, and Other Illnesses Perhaps Related to "Central Sensitization"'. Retrieved 12 December 2018 from <www.hsperson.com/pages/2May12.htm>

Aron, E. (2012b). *The Highly Sensitive Person* (blog) 'Ways to Deal with Serious Pain beyond Medication'. Retrieved 8 January 2019 from <www.hsperson.com/pages/1Feb12.htm>

Aron, E. (2013). *The Highly Sensitive Person* (blog) 'Fulfillment of a Dream – Vantage Sensitivity'. Retrieved 15 March 2019 from <hsperson.com/pages/1Feb13.htm>

Aron, E. (2015). *The Highly Sensitive Person* (blog) 'Emotional Regulation and HSPs'. Retrieved 17 March 2019 from <hsperson.com/emotional-regulation-and-hsps/>

Aron, E. (2016a). *The Highly Sensitive Person* (blog) 'Evidence for DOES'. Retrieved 12 March 2019 from <hsperson.com/faq/evidence-for-does/>

Aron, E. (2016b). *The Highly Sensitive Person* (blog) 'Is Sensory Processing (or Integration) Disorder (SPD) the same as Sensory Processing Sensitivity (SPS)?' Retrieved 7 June 2019 from <hsperson.com/faq/spd-vs-sps/>

Aron, E. & Aron, A. (1997). 'Sensory-Processing Sensitivity and its Relation to Introversion and Emotionality'. *Journal of Personality and Social Psychology*, 73(2).

Aron, E., Aron, A., & Davies, K. (2005). 'Adult Shyness: The Interaction of Temperamental Sensitivity and an Adverse Childhood Environment'. *Personality and Social Psychology Bulletin*, 31.

Aronson, D. (2009). 'Cortisol — Its Role in Stress, Inflammation, and Indications for Diet Therapy'. *Today's Dietitian*, 11(11).

Aspinall, P., Mavros, P., Coyne, R., & Roe, J. (2015). 'The Urban Brain: Analysing Outdoor Physical Activity with Mobile EEG'. *British Journal of Sports Medicine*, 49(4).

Benham, G. (2006). 'The Highly Sensitive Person: Stress and Physical Symptom Reports'. *Personality and Individual Differences*, 40(7).

Bernstein, A.J. (2001) *Emotional Vampires: Dealing with People who Drain You Dry*. New York: McGraw-Hill.

Black, R.A. (1998). *Broken Crayons: Break Your Crayons and Draw Outside the Lines*. Athens, GA: Cre8ng Places Press.

Bookofresearch.com. (2015). 'The Highly Sensitive Person (HSP) Explained'. Retrieved 16 March 2016 from <bookofresearch.wordpress.com/2015/02/28/the-highly-sensitive-person-hsp/>

Branden, Nathaniel (1994). *The Six Pillars of Self-Esteem*. New York: Bantam. (<NathanielBranden.com>)

Brindle, K., Moulding, R., Bakker, K., & Nedeljkovic, M. (2015). 'Is the Relationship Between Sensory-Processing Sensitivity and Negative Affect Mediated by Emotional Regulation?' *Australian Journal of Psychology*, 67 (4).

Harris, Theodore F. & Buck, Pearl S. (1971). *Pearl S. Buck: A Biography, Volume 1 – Her Philosophy as Expressed in Her Letters*. New York: The John Day Company.

Carson, S., Peterson, J. & M Higgins, D. (2003). 'Decreased Latent Inhibition Is Associated With Increased Creative Achievement in High-Functioning Individuals'. *Journal of Personality and Social Psychology*, 85.

Chen, X.Y., Rubin, K.H., & Sun, Y.R. (1992). 'Social Reputation and Peer Relationships in Chinese and Canadian Children: A Cross-Cultural Study'. *Child Development*, 63.

Cloud, H. & Townsend, J. (1992). *Boundaries: When to Say Yes, When to Say No to Take Control of Your Life*. Grand Rapids: Zondervan.

Cloud, H. & Townsend, J. (1995). *Safe People*. Grand Rapids: Zondervan.

Csikszentmihalyi, M. (1996). 'The Creative Personality: Ten Paradoxical Traits of the Creative Personality'. *Psychology Today*, July.

Csikszentmihalyi, M. (1997). *Creativity: Flow and the Psychology of Discovery and Invention*. New York: HarperCollins.

Dąbrowski, K. (1967). *Personality-Shaping Through Positive Disintegration*. Boston, Mass.: Little Brown.

Davis, J. (2004). *Psychological Benefits of Nature Experiences: An Outline of Research and Theory*. Boulder, Co.: Naropa University.

de Waal, F. (2009). *The Age of Empathy*. London: Souvenir Press.

Doherty-Sneddon, G., & Phelps, F.G. (2005). 'Gaze Aversion: A Response to Cognitive or Social Difficulty?' *Memory & Cognition*, 33(4).

Dweck, C.S. (2007). *Mindset: The New Psychology of Success*. New York: Ballantine.

Dweck, C.S. (2008). 'Can Personality be Changed?' *Current Directions in Psychological Science*, 17(6).

Evers, A., Rasche, J. & Schabracq, M.J. (2008). 'High Sensory-Processing Sensitivity at Work'. *International Journal of Stress Management*, 15(2).

Galanaki, E. (2005). 'Solitude in School: A Neglected Facet of Children's Development and Education'. *Childhood Education*, 81(3).

Goleman, D. (1995). *Emotional Intelligence*. New York: Bantam Books.

Gopnik, A. (2009). *The Philosophical Baby*. New York: Farrar Straus Giroux.

Hendrix, H. (1995). *Keeping the Love You Find*. London: Simon & Schuster.

Hendrix, H. (1988). *Getting the Love You Want*. New York: Harper & Row.

House, J.S., Landis, K.R., & Umberson, D. (1988). 'Social Relationships and Health'. *Science*, 241.

Howell, A.J., Dopko, R.L., Passmore, H., Buro, K. (2011). 'Nature Connectedness: Associations with Well-Being and Mindfulness'. *Personality and Individual Differences*, 51(2).

Jacobsen, M.E. (1999). *The Gifted Adult*. New York: Random House.

Jagiellowicz, J., Xu, X., Aron, A., Aron, E., Cao, G., Feng, T., & Weng, X. (2011). 'The Trait of Sensory Processing Sensitivity and Neural Responses to Changes in Visual Scenes'. *Social Cognitive and Affective Neuroscience*, 6(1).

Jung, C. (1923). *Psychological Types*. Harcourt Brace: New York.

Kaplan, S. (1995). 'The Restorative Benefits of Nature: Toward an Integrative Framework'. *Journal of Environmental Psychology*, 16.

Kaufman, S.B. & Gregoire, C. (2015). *Wired to Create: Unravelling the Mysteries of the Creative Mind*. New York: TarcherPerigee.

Keirsey, David; Bates, Marilyn (1984). *Please Understand Me: Character & Temperament Types* (Fifth ed.). Prometheus Nemesis Book Company: Carlsbad, CA.

Konrath, S., Meier, B.P., & Bushman, B.J. (2014). *Development and Validation of the Single Item Narcissism Scale (SINS)*. Public Library of Science (PLOS), 9(8).

Lee, R.M., Draper, M., & Lee, S. (2001). 'Social Connectedness, Dysfunctional Interpersonal Behaviours, and Psychological Distress: Testing a Mediator Model'. *Journal of Counseling Psychology*, 48(3).

Levine, A., & Heller, R. (2012). *Attached: The New Science of Adult Attachment and How It Can Help You Find and Keep Love*. New York: Penguin.

Linden, C. *Anxiety and Stress Relief Resources* (blog). 'Creative intellect as a marker for genetic predisposition to high anxiety conditions'. Accessed 1 July 2019 at <http://anxietyreliefsolutions.com/creative-intellect-as-a-marker-for-genetic-predisposition-to-high-anxiety-conditions/>

Lipton, B. (2007). *The Biology of Belief: Unleashing the Power of Consciousness, Matter, & Miracles*. New York: Hay House.

Lovecky, D. (1993). 'Creative Connections: Perspectives on Female Giftedness'. *Advanced Development Journal*, 5.

Lynn, C.D. (2014). 'Hearth and Campfire Influences on Arterial Blood Pressure: Defraying the Costs of the Social Brain Through Fireside Relaxation'. *Evolutionary Psychology*, 12(5).

Mayer, F.S., Frantz, C.M., Bruehlman-Senecal, E., & Dolliver, K. (2009). 'Why is Nature Beneficial? The Role of Connectedness to Nature'. *Environment and Behaviour*, 41.

McConnell, A.R., Brown, C.M., Shoda, T.M., Stayton, L.E., & Martin, C.E. (2011). 'Friends With Benefits: On the Positive Consequences of Pet Ownership'. *Journal of Personality & Social Psychology*, 101(6).

Mehl, M.R., & Vazire, S. (2010). 'Eavesdropping on Happiness: Well-being is Related to Having Less Small Talk and More Substantive Conversations'. *Psychological Science*, 21(4).

Montag C., Buckholtz J.W., Hartmann P., Merz M., Burk C., Hennig J., & Reuter M. (2008). 'COMT Genetic Variation Affects Fear Processing: Psychophysiological Evidence'. *Behavioural Neuroscience*, 122(4).

Noble, K. 'Kathleen Noble – An Interview by Douglas Eby'. Retrieved 22 February 2019 from <http://talentdevelop.com/interviews/KNoble.html>.

Pluess, M., & Belsky, J. (2012). 'Vantage Sensitivity: Individual Differences in Response to Positive Experiences'. *Psychological Bulletin*, 139(4).

Riley, L. (2015). 'Highly Sensitive Personality and Creativity'. Retrieved 9 May 2019 from <http://highlysensitive.org/325/highly-sensitive-personality-and-creativity/>

Rosetree, R. (2001). *Empowered by Empathy*. Stirling, VA: Women's Intuition.

Ryan, R.M., Weinstein, N., Bernstein, J., Warren Brown, K., Mistretta, L., & Gagné, M. (2010). 'Vitalizing Effects of Being Outdoors and in Nature'. *Journal of Environmental Psychology*, 30(2).

Salmon, P. (2001). 'Effects of Physical Exercise on Anxiety, Depression and Sensitivity to Stress – A Unifying Theory'. *Clinical Psychology Review*, 21(1).

Sartre, Jean-Paul (1989). *No Exit and Other Plays*. Penguin Random House, p. 45.

Schieman, S., & Turner, H.A. (2001). 'When Feeling Other People's Pain Hurts: The Influence of Psychosocial Resources on the Association Between Self-Reported Empathy and Depressive Symptoms'. *Social Psychology Quarterly*, 64(4).

Shin, J., Steger, M. & Henry, K. (2016). 'Self-Concept Clarity's Role in Meaning in Life Among American College Students: A Latent Growth Approach'. *Self and Identity*, 15(2).

Smith, R.L., & Rose, A.J. (2011) 'The "Cost Of Caring" in Youths' Friendships: Considering Associations Among Social Perspective Taking, Co-Rumination, And Empathetic Distress'. *Developmental Psychology*, 47(6).

Stress Management Society. (2015). 'What Is Stress?' Retrieved 17 November 2015 from <http://www.stress.org.uk/what-is-stress.aspx>

Sunil, K., & K.Y. Rooprai (2009). 'Role of Emotional Intelligence in Managing Stress and Anxiety at Workplace'. ASBBS Annual Conference: Las Vegas, 16(1).

Truitt, A. (1984). *Daybook: The Journal of an Artist*. New York: Penguin.

Vanzant, I. (1999). *In the Meantime*. New York: Simon & Schuster.

Ward, Deborah (2015). *Overcoming Low Self-Esteem with Mindfulness*. London: Sheldon Press.

Wilson et al. (2014). 'Just Think: The Challenges of the Disengaged Mind'. *Science*, July.

Weinstein, N., Przybylski, A.K. & Ryan, R.M. (2009). 'Can Nature Make Us More Caring? Effects of Immersion in Nature on Intrinsic Aspirations and Generosity'. *Personality And Social Psychology Bulletin*, 35(10).

Zabelina, D.L., O'Leary, D., Pornpattananangkul, N., Nusslock, R., & Beeman, M. (2015). 'Creativity and Sensory Gating Indexed by the P50: Selective Versus Leaky Sensory Gating in Divergent Thinkers and Creative Achievers'. *Neuropsychologia*, March (69).

Zeff, T. (2010). *The Strong, Sensitive Boy*. San Ramon, CA: Prana Publishing.

Index